# KING KLOPP

# KING KLOPP

## REBUILDING THE LIVERPOOL DYNASTY

### LEE SCOTT

First published by Pitch Publishing, 2020

Pitch Publishing
A2 Yeoman Gate
Yeoman Way
Worthing
Sussex
BN13 3QZ
www.pitchpublishing.co.uk
info@pitchpublishing.co.uk

A CIP catalogue record is available for this book
from the British Library.

ISBN 978 1 78531 650 0

Typesetting and origination by Pitch Publishing
Printed and bound in India by Replika Press Pvt. Ltd.

# Contents

For Kelly, Alex, Thomas and Harry.

Without your love and support, none of this would be possible.

# Introduction

The 2019/20 season presents something of a turning point in the history of Liverpool Football Club and the English Premier League. Liverpool won the title for the first time in 29 years as they broke a drought that had stretched since the 1980s. To a point, some Liverpool fans had begun to feel as though the club was cursed as season after season they contrived to find some way to underperform domestically. This culminated in the 2018/19 season when Liverpool finished in second place, behind Manchester City, despite winning 97 points and only losing one match and even the Champions League trophy was not enough to appease the fans.

For many teams and coaches, a disappointment of that magnitude would be difficult to overcome. Not for this Liverpool side, however, and we have seen why their coach Jürgen Klopp referred to the squad as *'mentality monsters'*. The 2019/20 season will go down in history as one that was particularly challenging despite the absolute dominance of Liverpool as they amassed an incredible 82 points from the first 29 matches of the season. That was, of course, the point at which football across the world ground to a halt due to the coronavirus pandemic. Liverpool were left needing just two more wins to secure their first-ever Premier League title, their last title win coming before the inaugural Premier League season, but there was a chance that the season would end up being cancelled altogether.

Luckily for Liverpool the league was allowed to restart, albeit behind closed doors, and they secured the title.

This, however, is not a book that will follow the narrative of this title win, although there are likely to be many others to follow that do so. Instead, we will take this Liverpool team and attempt to understand how they became one of the most efficient and effective units in the history of football, from a tactical point of view.

Here is the thing; despite the huge lead that they amassed over the course of the season, Liverpool were not entirely dominant. In some matches, they won by the tightest of margins but the key point is that they won and that they kept winning. The 2019/20 season represents something of a turning point for Liverpool as a football club and as a city. Gone were the mistakes that had littered previous campaigns and in their place came a new and visibly determined group of players.

Jürgen Klopp, in his own right, is a coach who deserves every success. His easy demeanour with players and the press makes him seem like a coach who achieves results through his man-management and ability to make all players feel as though they are a part of something bigger. Those that truly believe this, however, are failing to appreciate the tactical complexity of the sides that Klopp builds. This Liverpool team in itself has undergone transformations since Klopp's arrival in 2015. Now, we are seeing a Liverpool side that has undergone a continuous period of refinement to get to the level that we see today.

The purpose of this book is to break this Liverpool side down into their individual tactical components and to then explain the context behind each of these components. I believe that the appetite amongst football fans to consume and understand detailed content that revolves around tactical concepts and strategy is growing at an incredible rate, while football as a sport still offers the opportunity for people to consume and enjoy it through a multitude of lenses. Some want the passion and companionship of attending matches live and enjoying the spectacle as part of a crowd, others want to enjoy the game from the comfort of their own home as pure entertainment, while others prefer to break down and analyse the game from a tactical standpoint to understand what coaches are trying to achieve. It will come as no surprise to learn that I fall firmly into the latter bracket.

My aim is to provide the information in this book in a manner that is accessible to all of those that are interested in the tactical side of the game. There are some who will be reading this who are unsure as to whether this book is for them. I would encourage those people to read on and give it a chance. Some tactical writing could be easily mistaken as a piece of academic research with language used that appears to add levels of complexity beyond the normal football fan. I cannot state how much I do not believe that this is the case. We can describe the same tactical concepts using language that is accessible and understandable and that helps people see the game through a whole new lens.

Despite that, there are points in this book where you might be challenged from a tactical perspective and one of the terms that I will use, and make no apology for using, will be half-spaces.

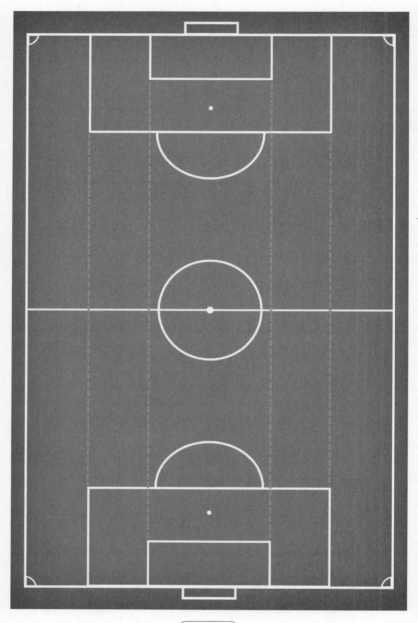

**Figure 1**

The half-space is a literal term that I find to be key in building tactical understanding. It is directly translated from German where the term was first popularised and refers to a fixed space, or rather spaces, on the pitch. We have provided an example of this in figure 1. You can see a football pitch that has been separated into five vertical sections. The two wide spaces and the central area are self-explanatory and what is left, areas 2 and 4 if you label them 1 to 5 from left to right. These spaces are the half-spaces. These areas of the pitch provide key tactical context when you are in possession as occupying these areas tends to force defensive players out of position.

As you will see throughout this book the ability to manipulate the opposition defensive structures and force them out of position is one of the key concepts that this Liverpool side is built around and this is part of the reason that Liverpool were able to break the streak and become the champions of the Premier League in 2019/20.

*Chapter 1*

# Trent Alexander-Arnold

For football fans, there are few more pleasing sights than that of a player making his first steps in the first team having developed at the club's own youth academy. Now, imagine that player went on, in the space of just a few years, to become one of the best players in the world in their position. That is the situation at the moment with Liverpool and their 21-year-old right-back Trent Alexander-Arnold.

When Alexander-Arnold first made the breakthrough at first-team level in 2016 there were few signs that the young full-back would develop into the player we see today. He played as an orthodox full-back and appeared to be lacking in the physicality that he would need to become a regular first-choice at the club. During his initial exposure to the first team, we saw the odd flash of the technical ability that would come to define him as a modern full-back but no more than that and, in retrospect, this should come as no surprise.

As a youngster in the Liverpool youth teams, Alexander-Arnold played in a variety of positions. He was a central defender, an attacking midfielder and a central midfielder at

14

various points but rarely a full-back. Indeed, the fact that the 21-year-old once stated that his preferred position was in the centre of the midfield leads some to feel that eventually he will move back into the centre of the pitch for club and country. As with many young players who are prodigiously talented at an early age there were issues around his attitude at times and he was easily wound up by the opposition for a period of time. Contrast that to the player that we see now, described by his coach Jürgen Klopp as *'one of the most relentless professionals I've met when it comes to focusing on getting better each and every day'*. Alexander-Arnold is a prime example of the dangers of labelling a young player early as a result of the normal growing process, whether mental or physical.

While there may be a logic in those calls for Alexander-Arnold to move into the centre of the midfield, many draw parallels to the skillset of the young full-back and that of Kevin De Bruyne of Manchester City, we have to consider the impact that move would have on the tactical structure of Liverpool as a whole. While for Manchester City we see De Bruyne act as the key ball progressor and creator from central areas and that is part of the overall game model for Pep Guardiola at the club, the picture is different for Liverpool. The 2019/20 season saw a firm move from Jürgen Klopp and his coaching team to use the midfield three, in their 4-3-3 system, in a functional rather than creative sense.

The 2019/20 season saw a significant development in the way in which Trent Alexander-Arnold was used in the Liverpool game model. This was a clear acknowledgement of the fact that the young right-back was now seen as a key creative force and progressor of the ball for his side.

To fully understand this change and why it was so important we have to understand the mechanisms and movements of the rest of the team as a whole. Everyone reading this book will be aware of the quality of the front three at Liverpool. The Senegalese attacker Sadio Mané occupies the left, the Brazilian forward Roberto Firmino is positioned centrally and then, and perhaps most importantly, the Egyptian Mohamed Salah plays from the right. At least those positional slots are what we see on the pre-match graphic that depicts the formation of either team. The positions occupied by these players are far more fluid with both Mané and Salah tending to move inside to either the half-spaces or the central areas. To allow these inverted movements from the wide forwards the central striker, Roberto Firmino, drops off into space traditionally occupied by a number '10' forming a loose triangle with the other two forwards.

These movements are designed to overload and confuse the opposition defence. Do the full-backs move inside to follow the wide forwards when they make their runs? Does one of the central defenders step out to follow Firmino when he drops into the deeper position? If the answer to either of these questions is yes then space is immediately created which can be exploited by other players in the Liverpool system moving forward from deeper positions. Of course, the opposition could simply drop into a narrow block with the full-backs tucking into the spaces beside the central defenders. To prevent this easy counter-movement Liverpool need to maintain their width in attack to force the full-backs to stay wider. This then creates the pockets of space that we see Liverpool use consistently as they move into the final third.

Traditionally this width would be offered by the full-backs who would both move high to occupy the opposition full-back and provide a wide outlet should the ball need to be played out to get in behind the defensive line. Indeed, this is still the case with Andrew Robertson on the left-hand side but not for Alexander-Arnold on the right-hand side.

In the 2019/20 season, we have seen Alexander-Arnold given a much freer role with the ability to move inside into positions that would normally be occupied by an inverted full-back. These movements see him take up positions centrally in areas in which we would typically expect to see a central midfielder. These movements from outside to inside change the angle of play that Alexander-Arnold has in possession and allow him to have a more direct influence on the game. This, of course, does not solve the issue of maintaining width on the right and with Salah and Alexander-Arnold both coming inside to play narrow the danger is that the centre of the pitch could become even more congested. To solve this issue Klopp came up with an inventive solution, the right-sided central midfielder, normally Jordan Henderson or Alex Oxlade-Chamberlain would pull out to the right side when Liverpool were in possession. This would stretch the opposition and create the space that Alexander-Arnold had when in possession of the ball.

This move to a different role for a player that is obviously the most important in the team from a creative standpoint is designed by Klopp and his staff to exert more control in games. When the German coach first arrived at Liverpool he did so surrounded by the narrative of *gegenpressing* and initial signs were that Klopp would look to implement his high tempo and aggressive pressing style of play. The 2019/20 season saw a move to something different. Pressing was still an extremely important part of their game out of possession but it was no longer quite as strongly part of the *identity* of Liverpool. Instead, they now look to dominate the game and control the tempo in a more efficient manner. With Alexander-Arnold now able to move inside to combine centrally Liverpool became far more effective in controlling the game and moving the ball until they found a passing lane that allowed them to penetrate into the opposition penalty area.

Over the course of the 2019/20 season Alexander-Arnold became one of the most efficient passers and effective playmakers in European football. His ability to access every area of the pitch through driven or floated passes explains the reasoning behind Klopp giving the young right-back such an important role within the team.

Before we delve further into the performance of Alexander-Arnold and the changes to his role in the 2019/20 season it can be helpful to use data to form a picture of the player and his performances for Liverpool.

The scatter graph in *figure 2* is designed to show players who progress the ball for their teams and who create high-quality chances. To do this I have created a metric called progressive actions per 90 minutes. This is a combination of two metrics from *Wyscout* called progressive runs and progressive passes per 90. The aim is to show which players progress the ball effectively into the opposition half and into the penalty area. The second metric is expected assists (xA) which is calculated in a similar way to the more well-known expected goals. This measures the likelihood that the chances created by each player would be converted into goals.

I have taken data from the top five European leagues and identified players who have played more than 1,000 minutes in the 2019/20 season. Straightaway we see two clear outliers in the data. The aforementioned

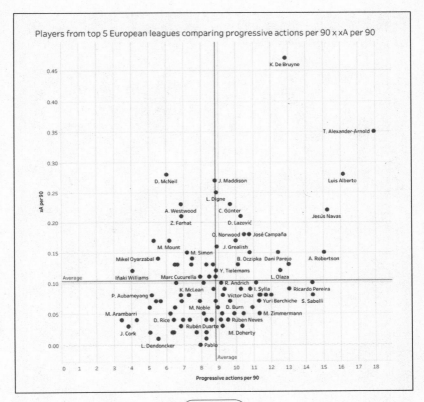

Figure 2

Kevin De Bruyne, of Manchester City, has an xA of over 0.45 per 90 minutes. To put this into context we can expect the Belgian international to directly assist one goal every two games. Then we have Alexander-Arnold with just under 18 progressive actions per game and an xA of 0.35 per match. With De Bruyne widely regarded as one of the best, if not the best outright, players in the Premier League then the data shows us that Alexander-Arnold is performing at a comparable level to the Belgian, despite being seven years younger.

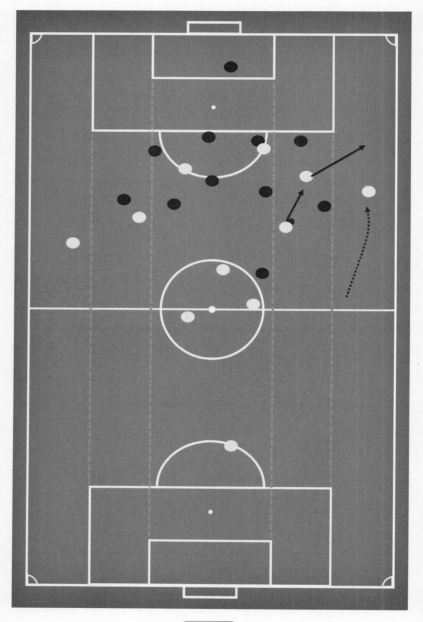

**Figure 3**

We touched upon this earlier in the chapter but *figure 3* gives a basic insight into the typical movements that we would see from a full-back in the attacking phase in a 4-3-3 structure. As the ball moves forward into the '8' in the right half-space we would then see the wide forward move inside to look for space to collect the ball.

This movement from the wide forward would empty the wide space and the full-back would move quickly to a high position to provide the width on that side of the field. When Alexander-Arnold first made his move into the first team these were the kinds of movements that we would see most often from him. We should acknowledge that even from these areas, as he does still at times make this movement should the situation arise, Alexander-Arnold poses a significant threat to the opposition with his ability to cross the ball. Indeed, he has already developed the ability to access the penalty area through a wide variety of crosses whether driven or curled into key zones. We see this crossing ability most prominently, however, when he is positioned just outside the corner of the penalty area and when the ball is set back to him. He has perfected the art of playing a curved looping cross to the far side of the penalty area that bypasses the opposition offside trap.

This traditional full-back role is of course perfectly fine in most cases. Indeed, up until this point Klopp had only ever used his full-backs in this sense. For the majority of his time at Borussia Dortmund, the right-back was the Polish international Lukasz Piszczek who was entirely dependable but not creative. Instead, the creative function was carried out by the three central midfielders as they took responsibility for progressing the ball and creating openings.

The challenge for Klopp coming into this season then was to find a way to unlock the creative powers of Alexander-Arnold.

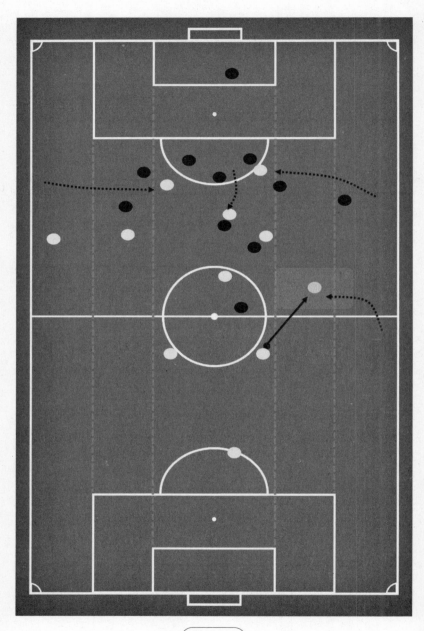

**Figure 4**

In *figure 4* we see an example of the kind of movement that we have seen more prominently from Alexander-Arnold in 2019/20. Early in the attacking phase, the ball is still at the feet of the right-sided central defender Joël Matip, and we see the front three making their rotational movements in the attack. Both Sadio Mané and Mohamed Salah move inside from the wide spaces while Roberto Firmino drops off the front line into a deeper position.

With these movements, we then see Alexander-Arnold moving inside, into the half-space, so that he can collect the ball from Matip in a pocket of space. As soon as he receives the ball in this area Alexander-Arnold will look to touch forward into space and progress the ball towards the opposition penalty area.

Here, we start to see the issues mentioned previously in the chapter. As Alexander-Arnold moves inside and collects possession we can see that the right-hand channel is now empty. This would allow the left-forward for the opposition to press Alexander-Arnold from one direction while a central midfielder pressed from a second angle. This is why there was a need for Liverpool to find a mechanism to stretch the field and pin the wide players out in the wide position.

From this position, however, Alexander-Arnold is now in a position to more effectively control the game.

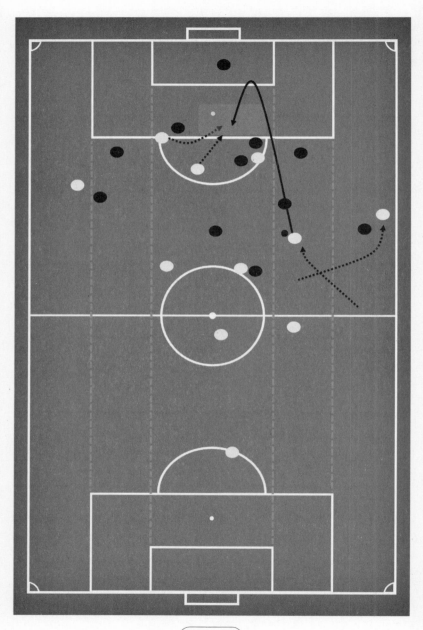

**Figure 5**

The difference in the position of Alexander-Arnold from playing as a traditional full-back or as an inverted full-back may be relatively slight, the difference between playing in the wide area or in the half-space, but the change of angle in the final third can be crucial for Liverpool when breaking down a deep defensive block.

In *figure 5* we see this in action with Alexander-Arnold in possession of the ball in the half-space although this time in an advanced position. An option to the outside has been provided by the movement of the right-sided central midfielder, Jordan Henderson, in this example and this prevents the wide player for the opposition from being able to move to close down the ball. From this position, there are a number of options available to Alexander-Arnold. He can play the easy pass outside to Henderson who is free to move forward into space or he can play the more difficult but potentially effective pass to access the penalty area. The young Englishman has the quality to consistently play passes from these angles that drop into the space between the defensive line and the goalkeeper. To be able to judge the weight of pass into these areas is a sign of a supremely gifted and technical footballer.

This is why we tend to see the attacking players for Liverpool constantly trying to lose their markers and move into space when Alexander-Arnold has possession of the ball in this area. They are looking for pockets of space in the defensive line that gives them separation from the defenders as they understand that the ball will be played perfectly into space and any advantage that they can get over the defenders will give them the optimum chance to get a shot on goal when the ball is played in. Another interesting feature of the Liverpool system that we see in this example is the position of the other two midfield players. They are on the same line behind the ball with Fabinho as the controlling midfielder and Georginio Wijnaldum positioned to his left, away from the ball. Wijnaldum is less of a vertical threat in terms of making runs but he positions himself perfectly to receive possession and play forward when Liverpool look to change the angle of the attack.

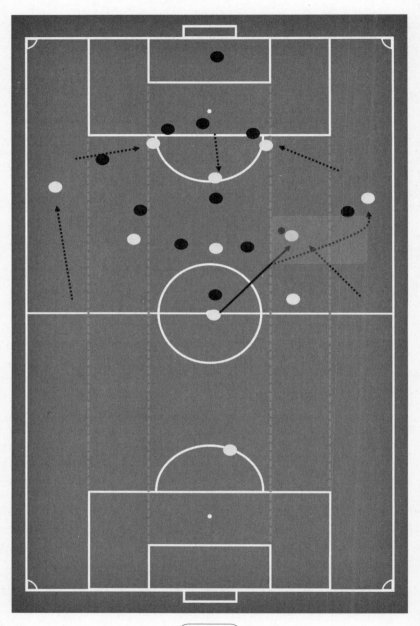

**Figure 6**

In *figure 6* we can see the full range of movements from Liverpool in this new-look structure. With the left-sided central defender, Virgil van Dijk, in possession at this moment we again see Alexander-Arnold making the same inverted movement to find room to receive the ball. This movement triggers the run from Jordan Henderson from his central position to the right-hand side of the pitch. Mohamed Salah and Sadio Mané both move inside and Roberto Firmino drops deep from the centre forward position to occupy a deeper role. On the left-hand side of the pitch, we immediately see Andrew Robertson move high to occupy the space emptied by the movement of Mané. In this snapshot, we see the balanced structure that Liverpool are able to build through different movements. The wide areas are occupied and they are positioned to overload the central spaces outside the penalty area.

Now, with Alexander-Arnold in possession of the ball we see the range of options and passing angles that these movements create. The wide area is open for a pass through to Henderson again but more interestingly there are angles to the feet of Mohamed Salah and Roberto Firmino to allow Liverpool to build into this overload in the central area of the pitch just outside the penalty area.

From this inverted position in the half-space Alexander-Arnold effectively becomes a pivot through which Liverpool can look to play. He occupies the pivot space, between the lines of the opposition attack and midfield, and dictates the tempo and direction of play from there.

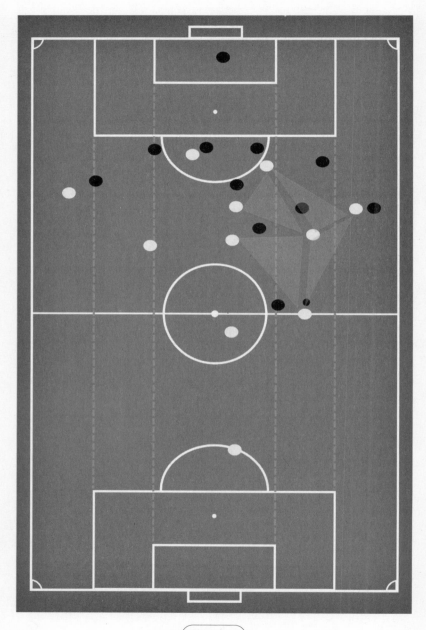

**Figure 7**

We see in *figure 7* an example of the importance of this pivot position to the overall Liverpool structure. With Alexander-Arnold inverted and in the half-space he is at the centre of a group of Liverpool players with five others arrayed around him. He is the key to the structure in that his positioning creates a series of triangles that allow the ball to be quickly shifted and the angle of the attack changed. This structure allows the ball to be progressed as soon as the passing lane to Mohamed Salah is open, inside from the right, and Roberto Firmino has dropped into the '10' space.

We see that Alexander-Arnold is positioned on the same line as the other two central midfielders, Fabinho and Georginio Wijnaldum, as Jordan Henderson has moved outside to the right-hand side. The structure and positioning of the Liverpool players has drawn the opposition in towards the ball to prevent them from becoming overloaded. This, in turn, creates an opportunity on the far side for the ball to be moved to a 1v1 situation in space.

It became a tool used by Liverpool more and more throughout the 2019/20 season for Alexander-Arnold to have possession before quickly switching the play via driven diagonal passes to the opposite full-back. From this position Wijnaldum is capable of moving forward to the clear space and Robertson, at left-back, is isolated 1v1 against the opposition. The key is that from this position and when in possession Alexander-Arnold controls the whole pitch.

## Chapter 2

# Defenders in possession

One of the most promising tactical changes that we have seen over the course of the last decade in football has been the rise in prominence of full-backs as they transition from purely functional defensive players to important progressors of the ball, this has already been discussed in chapter one. As with any change in the tactical norm of the game, however, this use of full-backs as an attacking outlet has led to a reaction from opposition coaches. While previously these players would enjoy time and space to receive the ball before moving forward, now they are closed down more quickly and have passing lanes cut off as opposition players move to negate their threat.

It stands to reason then that coaches would look for alternatives for progressing the ball up the field and the most logical option is to use central defenders in this manner. There have always been players who played in the centre of the defence and were considered *good* passers. Think back to when Alan Hansen played for the all-conquering Liverpool side of the 1970s and 1980s and the praise that he gained as a ball-playing centre back. If, however, nostalgia was to grab you and you were to seek out footage of the aforementioned Hansen playing in his prime you would be struck by how different the game looked then. Yes, Hansen steps out in possession and carries the ball into the opposition half and yes he is capable of playing long diagonal passes but he is doing so under little or no pressure as mechanisms like high pressing and pressing traps were all but unheard of at the time.

This Liverpool team, however, very much do use their central defenders as integral parts of their game model when they are in the attacking phase. This is something that should not come as a surprise to us given the fact that Jürgen Klopp has done the same thing at his previous clubs. When Klopp left Mainz to join Borussia Dortmund in 2008 one of the first things that he did was to return to Mainz to sign the Serbian central defender Neven Subotic. He went on to pair Subotic with Mats Hummels who was signed from Bayern Munich, originally on loan and later permanently, and these two went on to play key roles in the success that Dortmund experienced under Klopp. Both were excellent defensively but more than capable of handling possession of the ball when needed. Mats Hummels, in particular, has built a career on his ability to progress the ball accurately and decisively into the opposition half of the field.

If this type of central defensive partnership could thrive in the German Bundesliga, which was enjoying the *gegenpressing* revolution, then logic dictates that the same could be applied to the English Premier League where the pace of the game was perhaps higher but the pressing strategies of various clubs tended to be less sophisticated and less effective.

The trick, of course, would be finding the correct balance between the two players who would play at the centre of the defence and play such an influential role when Liverpool had possession of the ball. It goes without saying that the decision to continuously pursue the Dutch international Virgil van Dijk, despite protestations from his club at the time Southampton, and to complete the signing in January 2018 was a masterstroke but the Dutch defender had already shown during his time with Southampton, and to a lesser extent Celtic, that he fitted the profile of a ball-playing defender perfectly. The decision to return to Germany to sign the Cameroonian defender Joël Matip on a free transfer from Schalke, however, was a shrewd signing. Although given the German connection to the deal there is no doubt that Klopp would already have been well aware of the qualities that Matip would bring to the club the deal would also have met the criteria of the highly regarded transfer committee that is headed by the club's sporting director Michael Edwards. Alongside Van Dijk and Matip, we have also seen Klopp use the young English defender Joe Gomez and the more experienced Croatian Dejan Lovren at the heart of the defence. While Lovren is seen this season as a fourth-choice option we have seen Matip and Gomez battle one another for the position as the right-sided central defender where they would partner Virgil van Dijk on the opposite side.

With the players in place though, we also have to consider how they are used and what their role has been for Liverpool over the course of the 2019/20 season.

In the defensive phase, the role of the central defender for Liverpool is clear and the defensive side of the game is not one that we should disregard when discussing the role of the central defender in the Liverpool tactical system. They, of course, have to be able to defend their penalty area and they have to be able to track and mark their direct opponents but the role of a defender in modern football is far more nuanced than that and the teams' overall style of play plays a significant role.

When discussing how Liverpool have to defend we have to take an overall view and consider the way that they play in possession of the ball. We know that Liverpool tend to be dominant in terms of possession and this means that most of their games are played in the opposition half. As you will see later in this chapter this means that the defenders in the Liverpool system tend to push high up when in the attack phase and they operate as a release valve should the ball have to be played back to be switched to the other side. We also know that when Liverpool lose possession high up the field they will immediately look to counter-press in order to win the ball back and this press is aggressively pursued.

These two things alone tell us what the Liverpool central defenders need to be able to do in order to fit the Liverpool system. When the opposition wins the ball back, often in their own half, they will have to play quickly if they want to break the inevitable Liverpool press, which leads to more long passes being played by the opposition than you would otherwise expect. Given the fact that we know that the two Liverpool central defenders occupy a high area of the field when they are in possession, this means that they have to be comfortable defending when isolated against an opposition striker and running back towards their own goal as these direct passes will often be hit into the space between them and the goalkeeper. They also have to be capable of performing well in aerial duels as a proportion of these direct passes will lead to an aerial duel between the central defenders and the opposition strikers.

In order to understand more fully what a central defender is expected to do in the Liverpool system, we have to examine their roles when Liverpool are in possession. We have already discussed above that the central defenders are positioned high (further up the field) when Liverpool are in the attack and if for some reason the attack stalls then the ball will be switched back, often through the central defenders or the '6', and composure on the ball is a key asset for playing this position. As the 2019/20 season progressed we also saw the central defender, and Van Dijk in particular, used more often to progress the ball. As discussed earlier in the chapter, there is a move towards this function for defensive players, and as teams began to close down Trent Alexander-Arnold, at right-back, more often we saw the two central defenders entrusted with the ball both driving forwards with it at their feet and looking for the critical line-breaking passes that can lead to the creation of goalscoring opportunities. These progressive passes and runs were more and more critical as opposition teams dropped into deeper and deeper blocks in order to attempt to negate the threat posed by the Liverpool attacking line. It is not uncommon to see Van Dijk, Matip or Gomez stepping out of the defence and forcing the opposition to move to close the ball down. This simple action is designed to break the opposition defensive structure and as a player moves to close down the central defenders and prevent the ball from being progressed, they create space behind them. This space can then be exploited by movements from the more advanced Liverpool players.

Of course, while the ability to pass and drive the ball forward is important it is also essential that they understand when to play forwards and when to shift the ball across in order to change the angle of the attack. The key to this decision-making lies in the understanding and use of vertical passing lanes. When in possession you will often see the central defenders occupy the half-spaces of the pitch and their first instruction is to progress the ball through the thirds via vertical progressive passes. If this pass is not on then the ball will be switched across to the other central defender as they attempt to open a passing lane. The intention is to play the pass with enough pace that the defensive block does not have time to shift across and therefore the receiving player is able to take possession and play forwards.

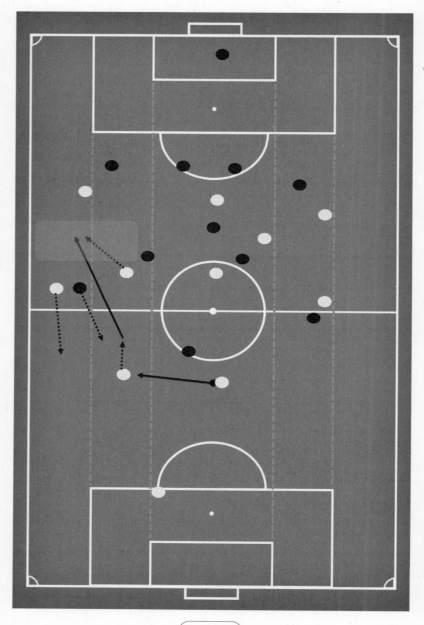

**Figure 8**

In *figure 8* we start to see the importance of the central defenders being capable and comfortable when bringing the ball out of the defence. While Liverpool are positioned in their normal 4-3-3 system, we see the start of the rotational movement they make with Alexander-Arnold moving into the half-space and Mohamed Salah doing the same further forward; the opposition are positioned in 4-1-4-1 shape with little space for Liverpool to take advantage of.

Joël Matip is originally in possession as the right-sided central defender and there is no easy passing option available to him. As such he opens up and plays a quick pass laterally to the feet of Virgil van Dijk. Again, the pace of the pass is important here as a slower pass would allow the opposition forward player to simply shift across and apply pressure to Van Dijk and the opportunity to play forward would be lost. This kind of passing movement also highlights why it is so useful to have a left-footed player as the left-sided central defender, and a right-footed player as the right-sided central defender. As the ball is moved across Van Dijk automatically receives on his stronger left foot, the foot furthest from the pressing opponent, and he can open his body to touch ahead. A right-footed player taking possession of the ball in this position would touch back towards the pressing player and cut off the space that they had to play in.

In our example, Van Dijk receives perfectly and can look to play forward. Initially, there is no clear option with which to progress the ball and Van Dijk moves forward towards the halfway line in possession of the ball. As he makes this movement we very quickly see space begin to open up for the Dutch defender. As the ball was passed across, the left-back, Andrew Robertson dropped back to make an angle for the pass outside and the right midfielder for the opposition moved with him. This right midfielder now has to move to engage the ball to prevent Van Dijk from breaking the line with a dribble.

The line in this instance refers to the line of four opposition midfield players that are stretched across the pitch. If the ball progresses past this line then five players, the forward and the four midfielders are effectively taken out of the game.

As the right midfielder moves to engage and press then he leaves space in behind. The central midfielder ahead of Van Dijk, Georginio Wijnaldum in this instance, recognises this space and makes a quick movement away from his marker to access this space. The ball is then easily played forward into space and Liverpool have an advanced platform from which they can launch the next phase of the attack.

Recognising that every attacking action creates space somewhere on the pitch is something that this Liverpool side do extremely well.

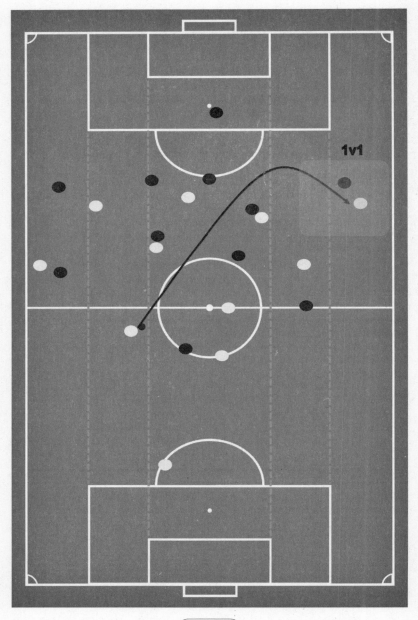

**Figure 9**

The increase in the amount of time that central defenders have in possession of the ball in the modern game means that they have to have a range of passing that can take advantage of space wherever it may be. While, as we have already discussed, the first aim of the defensive players when in possession in these areas is to pass forward and break the lines of the opposition, this is not always possible.

One of the most impressive aspects of Liverpool's performances in possession is that they are unpredictable in how and when they will attack. This is in part because they have one of the most versatile attacking units in football with Sadio Mané, Roberto Firmino and Mohamed Salah all comfortable receiving the ball in a variety of scenarios and under heavy pressure.

We see an example of this in *figure 9* with Virgil van Dijk once again in possession of the ball and Liverpool in their 4-3-3 as opposed to 4-1-4-1 for the opposition. It should be noted here that formations are not important but the occupation of space dictated by that formation is. The 4-1-4-1, for example, is a 4-3-3 when the opposition are in possession as the two wide midfielders push forward to support the striker. In the defensive phase though, these two wide players drop back to the midfield line to form a more effective defensive block.

Here, there is little space for Liverpool to play forward into but, on the far side of the pitch, Mohamed Salah has managed to isolate himself wide on the right against the defensive player. Given the quality of Salah's performances since he moved back to England to join Liverpool it is rare that he finds himself in a 1v1 situation like this.

As Van Dijk receives the ball he has time and space; again we are seeing central defenders given more space these days than players in other positions, and he has the vision and the range of passing to be able to quickly move the ball out of his feet to stretch the play and completely change the angle of the attack. With the diagonal pass, Liverpool are able to create an opportunity with Salah isolated against an opposition player while taking six opposition players out the game with a single pass.

The ability to change the point of attack and vary pass length in this manner makes it very difficult for the opposition to effectively defend against the Liverpool attack.

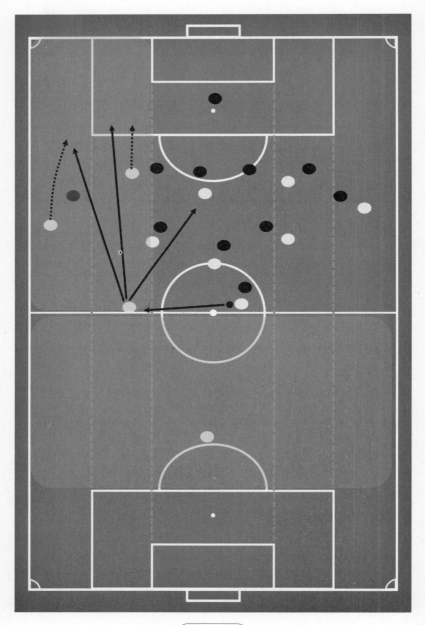

**Figure 10**

We have seen now the importance for Liverpool for their defenders to be able to progress the ball through dribbling or passing the ball and to be able to quickly change the angle and point of attack through vertical passing. For a team that tends to dominate possession and play on the front foot though, it is extremely important that the central defenders can handle the ball in tighter spaces in the opposition half.

So often we see Liverpool playing in the opposition half having forced the opposition back into a deep and compact block and in *figure 10* we see one such example. Once again the sequence starts with the right-sided central defender, Joe Gomez this time, as he has received the ball back from Trent Alexander-Arnold who is on the right-hand side. When Gomez takes possession the defensive block is still positioned to stop the ball from progressing cleanly; remember progressing the ball is the first priority here, and once again it is switched back across to the left where Virgil van Dijk is positioned in the half-space.

Once again we see that when Van Dijk receives the ball in this area the defensive block has not had the time to shift across and cut off the space that the Dutch defender can pass into. There are three passing options open to Van Dijk when the ball is moved across. He can play out to the left and behind the right-back of the opposition for Robertson to move on to. He can attempt the vertical pass straight ahead that is more difficult but likely to release Sadio Mané into the penalty area or he can play into the feet of Roberto Firmino. In this example, the pass went into Firmino centrally and Liverpool broke through when the Brazilian forward collected the ball and played through to Salah in the right half-space.

We also see in this example the space behind the two central defenders that we have highlighted to give an insight into how much of the pitch they have to control should the opposition win the ball and be able to transition quickly to attack.

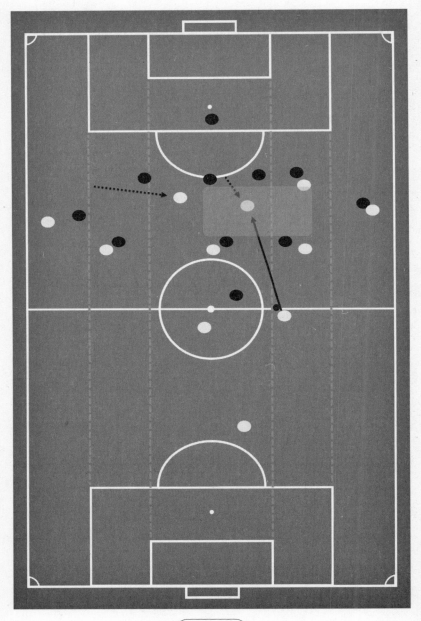

**Figure 11**

We have already touched upon the fact that progressing the ball vertically and breaking the lines of the opposition is the first priority for defensive players when they take possession of the ball, and in *figure 11* we have an example that displays this perfectly.

We see this example as Joël Matip has possession of the ball.

Before the pass can be played and break the line though, there has to be some movement from the Liverpool attacking players to create separation and a pocket of space that they can play in and receive the pass. Initially, Roberto Firmino is positioned against the far-sided central defender. We then see Sadio Mané making a run from the left-hand side that moves across this central midfielder leaving him effectively with two Liverpool players to pick up. The movement from outside to inside from Mané, however, triggers a rotation and Firmino immediately drops off the front line towards the ball.

This movement from the forward creates the opportunity and Matip is able to quickly fire a pass through the defensive line for the forward to take possession in an area that allows him to turn and threaten the penalty area.

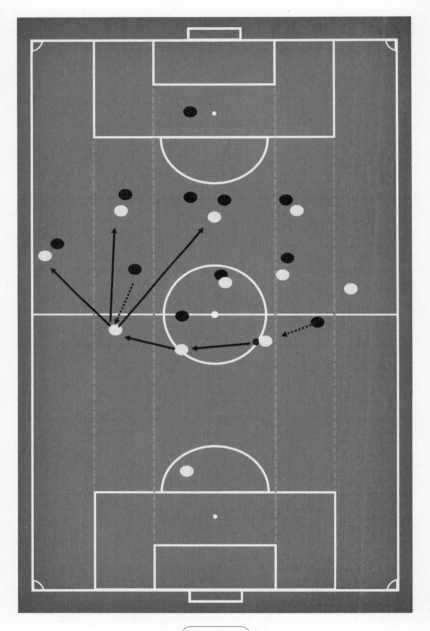

**Figure 12**

The basic principle of progressing the ball from the central defenders is to have a numerical superiority compared to the defensive side that are pressing you. In other words, if there is one defensive player pressing and engaging the ball then you should have two central defenders. This means that if the opposition pushes two defensive players forward in order to press and engage then you need to find a solution to allow the ball to still progress cleanly.

Liverpool use a simple answer to this problem as we see in *figure 12*. With the opposition positioned in a 4-4-2, it would be 4-1-4-1 but the left midfielder has moved to engage the ball and press the defender from behind, so there is no clear avenue to progress the ball.

To solve this and create a numerical superiority of 3v2 we see the Dutch midfielder Wijnaldum drop back from his position in the centre of the midfield to form a chain of three with the two central defenders. This simple movement to a deeper line from the midfielder changes the structure of the build-up completely and despite the pressure from the two opposition players Liverpool are still able to create a situation where they have possession of the ball in a deep position with the capacity to progress cleanly into dangerous areas. As Wijnaldum takes possession he, as above, has three clear passing options: out to Robertson, forward to Mané or diagonally to Firmino and as the opposition have committed so many men forward they are less compact defensively as the ball is played forward.

**Figure 13**

For all that Liverpool use their central defenders as a key tool to progress the ball, they are not infallible and over the course of the 2019/20 season we saw one team find a way to negate their effectiveness and to stop Liverpool from being as effective in possession. The group stage of the 2019/20 Champions League saw Liverpool up against Napoli, Red Bull Salzburg and Gent, and despite the challenge of playing against the intensity of the Austrian side, it was Napoli that provided the stiffest test.

They played a strict 4-4-2 in both the home and away legs and out of possession the two forward players were instructed to stay as close to the two Liverpool central defenders as possible. With the rest of the Napoli side arrayed in a compact block with little or no space between the lines, Liverpool struggled to create the angles or opportunity to play beyond the block and then create opportunities.

As Napoli then regained possession, the two forward players were ideally positioned to make sharp runs in behind for direct passes into space.

This system is not, however, without risk and the Italian side displayed a great deal of discipline to hold their compact defensive block when they were at constant risk of being overloaded as Liverpool swept forward with possession. Given the important role that the central defenders have for Liverpool in progressing the ball though, it is surprising that we have not seen more teams line up in a similar structure to take away the effectiveness of the central defenders in possession.

## Chapter 3
# The importance of the '6'

In the preceding chapters, we have already touched upon the fact that there was a definite move from Jürgen Klopp and his coaching staff towards exercising more control over games in a tactical sense. There was a definite and significant move away from the chaos-centred approach that Klopp had initially implemented when he moved to England. But was there? There is still an element of chaos in the attacking game model that we have seen Liverpool implement in the 2019/20 season. Consider the prescribed rotations and movement that we have already described in earlier chapters. The lone forward drops deep and this allows the two wide forwards to move centrally. The movement of the wide forwards inside creates space in the wide areas and the left-back moves high to occupy this space. On the right-hand side, the right-back moves into the half-space but this creates an issue with width on the right and so the right-sided central midfielder rotates out. All of these movements create chaos both in terms of the occupation and creation of space and in terms of the stress that they put on the opposition defensive structure.

So instead of describing the general structure that Liverpool employ in possession as *chaos* perhaps *organised chaos* is more effective. These movements are organised because they are so well embedded in the players through work on the training field. We as onlookers already understand the movements that the Liverpool players are going to make and the opposition will have the same information. It is one thing, however, to know what they are going to do but it is another thing altogether to stop this Liverpool team.

With all of the movements and rotations across the pitch though, it is important to have a player who is still able to add a sense of calmness and control to the match. In this Liverpool team, that role falls to the '6' or the single pivot at the base of the midfield three.

There have been three players over the course of the 2019/20 season who have fulfilled this role for Liverpool. The 26-year-old Brazilian international Fabinho is the first choice for the role but both Georginio Wijnaldum and Jordan Henderson have spent time as the single pivot over the course of the season as well.

There are, of course, different ways that teams can use a player in the pivot position. Traditionally the deepest of three midfielders would fulfil a purely defensive role with their aim being to disrupt the opposition attacks before retaining the ball through safe passes. Gradually we saw the introduction of the deep playmaker in the pivot position whose role was to circulate possession of the ball. The choice to move the playmaker from his more traditional slot as one of the two more advanced midfielders in a three was designed to create more space for the playmaker to receive the ball and then play progressively.

For Liverpool in the 2019/20 season, we saw a combination of these two roles with the player in this role expected to be able to contribute in both the defensive and attacking phases of the game.

The role is integral to the way that Liverpool play, both in and out of possession, and it is indicative that one of Klopp's most trusted assistants, Pepjin Lijnders, described Fabinho as being the key to controlling space and therefore the game for Liverpool.

In an interview for the website Liverpoolfc.com following a 2-1 win over Spurs at Anfield, Lijnders said: *'He needs to be the one who protects us constantly, he is controlling a very important space for counter-attacks. He does that as nobody else, that's why I called him "the lighthouse" – he guides us. He controls that space as nobody else.'* This is a key insight into the role that the pivot player has to play in this Liverpool side. As the attacking rotations take place and space is occupied and overloaded in the final third, there is, of course, a natural reaction to this in that if there is a counter-attack as the opposition attack in transition then there will be space in the Liverpool half which will be exploited. The attacking movements of the left-back, high and wide, and the right-back, into the half-space, means that the wide spaces are left open. This is countered slightly via the recruitment of central defenders who are mobile and capable of defending when isolated in wide spaces as the ball is played forward quickly in transition, but there is another effective way to manage this issue.

This space can also be defended by the pivot as that player has the capacity to move left or right in order to negate the spaces that the opposition may try to attack into. Fabinho is uniquely suited to this role given the fact that his initial exposure to European football saw him play as a right-back for both Rio Ave in Portugal and Real Madrid Castilla in Spain. When he made the move to Monaco in 2013 we saw the Brazilian moved to play either in the centre of the defence or at the base of the midfield.

This tactical versatility that Fabinho possesses along with his mobility learnt as an attacking full-back means that he can cover the entire width of the pitch with ease. The defensive profiles of the other two players who have occupied the '6' role are slightly different. The Dutch international Wijnaldum excels when defending and blocking passing lanes with his understanding of angles and body positioning but is far less mobile than Fabinho. Jordan Henderson, on the other hand, is extremely mobile and he performs extremely well defensively in chaos. In situations when more control is required, however, Henderson can be exposed. While these different profiles offer tactical variation to Klopp and his staff there is, without a shadow of a doubt, an option that is far better than the others and this is playing Fabinho as the '6'. The Brazilian international exudes confidence and calmness that is incredibly important with the chaos of the rotations and movement around him. With Liverpool transitioning to a model of *controlled chaos* in the 2019/20 season there is no doubt whatsoever that Fabinho provides the control, along with Virgil van Dijk in the centre of the defence.

So, we are not aware of the requirements for the '6' or pivot in the Liverpool system when they do not have possession of the ball but what about in possession? We have to keep in mind after all the fact that Liverpool enjoy the majority of the possession in almost every match they play; this is, of course, a reaction to the ability of Liverpool to attack quickly in transition with their world-class front three. Teams drop deeper and are more passive in their defensive phase because they are concerned about leaving space behind their defensive line that could be exploited.

The general positioning of the pivot for Liverpool remains central. That player plays a similar role to the central defenders albeit from a more advanced position in that they act as a release point for the ball to travel back from one side of the pitch before being switched back through to the other side, but there is more to the role than that and this is where Fabinho really comes into his own. Liverpool use the pivot periodically as a tool to break the lines of the opposition through delayed forward movements that are difficult to effectively defend against. These movements tend to come against deep and compact defensive blocks when Liverpool are in the second or even third phases of their attack, which means that the initial attacking movement was repelled and Liverpool had to reset the ball to try again to find a route through the defence. When this happens we can see the pivot player step forward to form a more active piece of the attacking structure. If we consider the moving pieces that the opposition are already having to defend against – the wide forwards moving from outside to inside while the forward moves from high to low; the left-back has moved high and the right-back is threatening an overload in the half-space – now, we have a player who in Fabinho's case is over 6ft tall making a late run towards the edge of the penalty area with a movement that is exceptionally difficult to stop. These vertical movements that add another direction through which Liverpool can break defences down are effective in creating quick situations in which the defensive line can be overloaded and broken through.

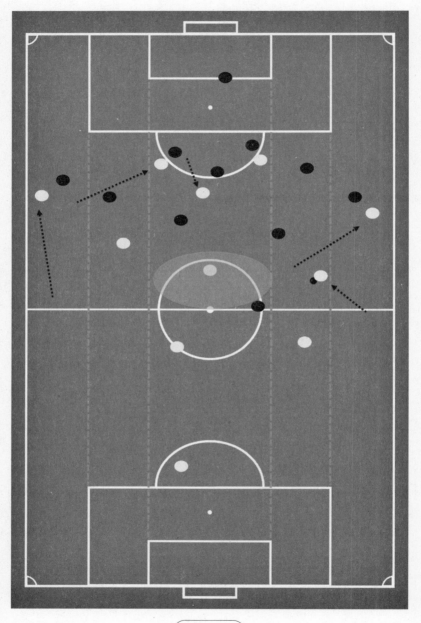

Figure 14

In *figure 14* we begin to see the importance of having a player occupy a central position to form a reference point for the rest of the team. With the ball having travelled into the right half-space where Trent Alexander-Arnold has positioned himself we start to see the familiar patterns of movement into the final third. As Roberto Firmino drops into a deeper position both wide forwards move inside to occupy the attention of the central defenders. These movements, of course, pin the defensive players and prevent them from following Firmino out into space.

Width is provided on the left side by Andrew Robertson moving high into the opposition half while Jordan Henderson rotates to the wide space on the right-hand side of the field.

While all of this is happening Fabinho retains his position in the centre of the field. This is crucial, of course, should Alexander-Arnold attempt to play a pass into the final third or penalty area which is then intercepted as Fabinho can quickly provide cover for his team-mates that have moved into advanced positions.

The interesting thing in this Liverpool side is that there are two key pivot players that form the reference points for the side in the attacking phase. One is Firmino when he plays as the '9' and drops off the front line, where he looks to take up central positions through which the ball can be played; the other is the '6' and in particular Fabinho. The importance of having players occupy the central areas should never be taken for granted, especially amidst all of the movement in and out of the half-spaces.

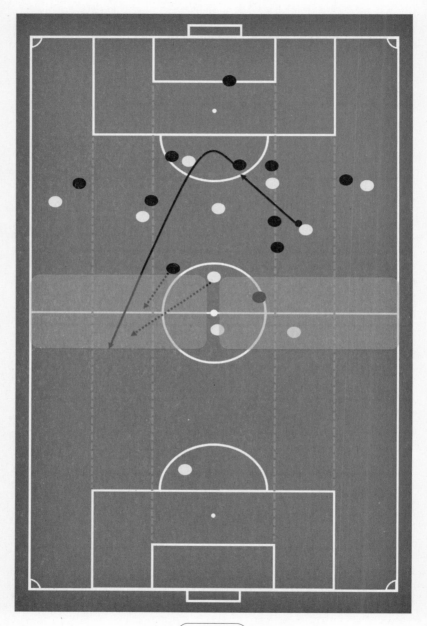

**Figure 15**

Having a player, in Fabinho especially, who has exceptional mobility in the '6' role can be important purely based on the tendency for attacking structures to be heavily distributed on the ball side of the pitch.

We see an example of this in *figure 15* with the ball again situated in the half-space, although this time Alex Oxlade-Chamberlain is in possession with Alexander-Arnold having moved to a higher position on the outside. You can clearly see that the overall structure for Liverpool has rotated over to the ball side of the field. This is clearly evident when we look at the positioning of the central defenders with both being positioned over to the right-hand side. This is perfectly normal and the two defenders, on the first line, are positioned in this manner to provide a release valve for the ball should the attacking movement break down. This would see the ball being played back into the central defenders before it could then be shifted across towards the opposite side of the field.

This positioning, although a normal occurrence, can still be problematic given the lack of cover on the weak side of the pitch should the opposition win the ball back and be able to launch their own attack in transition.

This is what we see here with Oxlade-Chamberlain looking in the first instance to play the ball into the edge of the penalty area only for the opposition to win the ball back. They then look to transition quickly with a direct pass to the weak side that sees one of their midfielders looking to run on to the ball in space.

Now, Liverpool are fortunate that they have central defenders who possess great pace. Virgil van Dijk, Joe Gomez and Joël Matip are all capable of covering the ground and defending when isolated in these areas. With Fabinho playing as the '6', however, this is not necessary as the Brazilian quickly adjusts to become active in the defensive phase. In being capable of defending in these zones the '6' then provides a more balanced defensive structure with the two central defenders able to defend the centre, and the ball near-side of the pitch. This prevents the opposition from being able to transition quickly before pulling the defenders towards the ball and switching play back across to create attacking overloads.

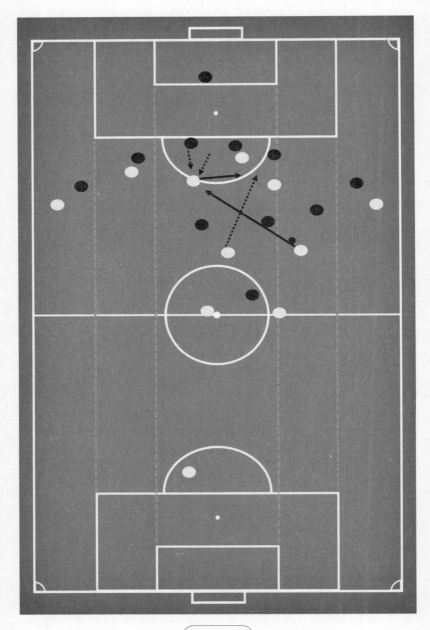

**Figure 16**

While the defensive capacity of the player in the '6' role for Liverpool is, of course, important, the player in question has an impact in the attacking phase. We have already discussed earlier in the chapter the importance of this player being able to join in the attack through delayed runs that cause chaos and create overloads that can break through the opposition defensive structure.

We see an example of how this works in *figure 16* as the play is being built up once again in the right half-space, this time with Jordan Henderson. The key to the success of the attacking movement is the movement off of the highest line of Firmino as he looks to receive the ball. This time, however, one of the opposition central defenders elects to follow the Brazilian as he moves down into the '10' space and this creates the opportunity for Liverpool to create the overload in this zone.

As the pass is played into the feet of Firmino we see that with Mané, positioned in the left half-space, and Salah, positioned centrally, Liverpool are well placed to take advantage of the space in the defensive line that has been created by the movement of the defender to track the run made by Firmino. To add to this threat we then see Fabinho making a vertical run, from the '6' space.

As Firmino receives the ball we see that Fabinho has timed the run perfectly and the ball can simply be played into his path. Now, with Mané and Salah essentially pinning their closest defenders back, as neither defender is willing to leave the dangerous attackers given their ability to explode into space, we see that Liverpool have created an overload in the centre of the opposition defensive block.

As Fabinho collects possession of the ball his momentum allows him to break through the defensive line to create an opportunity at goal.

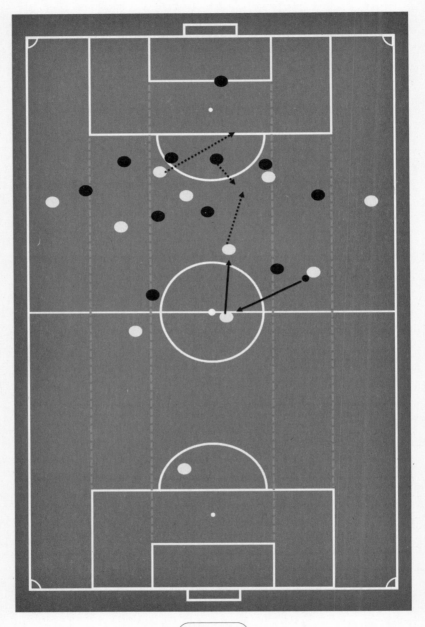

**Figure 17**

While the ability of the '6' in the Liverpool system to create these overloads in the highest line provides opportunities to penetrate into the opposition penalty area they also play a key role in breaking lines further back to aid with the progression of the ball. In *figure 17* we see a clear example of this with Liverpool trying to break down a team that are playing in a compact block with an initial 4-5-1 structure.

One of the issues that sides face when they try to press possession-heavy teams with only one forward player is that in order to press more effectively they tend to have to commit deeper players to the pressing action.

We see this clearly in the example above as Liverpool are in comfortable possession. The ball is initially with Alexander-Arnold in the right-back slot while the pressing forward player is still positioned closer to the left-sided central defender. This triggers one of the opposition players to move out of the midfield line in order to put pressure on the ball carrier. As the ball initially moves back to Joël Matip, the right-sided central defender, we then see that the midfield player who has moved to engage with the press is caught essentially in a poor position.

The ball can then be progressed cleanly into Fabinho, playing again as the '6', in a position in which he can collect the ball and then exploit the space that has been created by the opposition midfielder moving out of his positional slot. This is a key function of the '6' in this new-look Liverpool system that was implemented in the 2019/20 season. While, as we have already discussed, the '6' provides the control that balances the chaos, the players that are entrusted with this position and role also have to be able to break from this controlled role to add to the chaos in terms of breaking the lines of the opposition when the opportunity presents itself.

This is evident from this example as Fabinho collects possession of the ball and we can see that the line of the opposition's midfield has been stretched and broken by the player moving out to press. Fabinho drives through this space and then forces one of the defenders to react in order to engage with the ball.

As the defender moves to engage Fabinho this creates another gap in the defensive block, this time in the defensive line, and on this occasion, it was Firmino who moved to exploit this space with a diagonal movement, as Mané had dropped into a deeper position.

The ability and willingness of Liverpool players to break lines in this manner is key for them as more and more of the opposition that they face are willing to sit in a deep block to deny them the space to play in the final third. By pulling players out of their defensive slots, as we have seen twice in this example, Liverpool are then capable of creating opportunities to penetrate into the key areas around the penalty area.

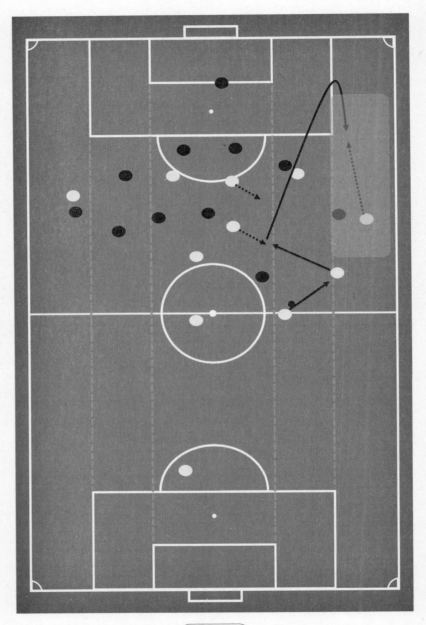

**Figure 18**

While being able to control space and then join the attacking phase to create opportunities against deep defensive blocks, the player in the '6' role also has a key role to play in creating angles to combine with players in order to aid the progression of the ball.

We see an example of this in *figure 18* with Jordan Henderson this time playing in the '6' role. Once again the ball is being progressed on the right-hand side, although this time it is Joe Gomez who is playing in the right-back position and, of course, Gomez is less of a threat in terms of ball progression than Alexander-Arnold.

As is normal we see Firmino dropping towards the ball to provide a passing option, but Gomez is less likely to play this line-breaking pass, instead Henderson, as the '6', moves towards the ball to shorten the connection between the two players.

This movement allows Gomez to simply play the lateral pass to the feet of Henderson who then plays the progressive pass himself over the heads of the midfield line to find Oxlade-Chamberlain who is positioned in the right-midfield role at that time.

It is interesting to note again that the positioning of the far-sided central midfielder, Wijnaldum, has him on the same line as the '6'. Once again the midfield is more functional than creative but this creates a solid base from which Liverpool can play in the attacking phase.

## Chapter 4

# Pressing as a playmaker

When Jürgen Klopp made the decision to move to England and sign a contract with Liverpool in 2015 the excitement around the Premier League was palpable. Although Klopp's time at Borussia Dortmund ended on something of a low note he was still considered one of the most capable and likeable coaches in football.

Central to this sense of excitement was the expectation that Klopp would look to implement his famous *gegenpressing* style in the English game. Whilst there may have been signs of this initially, however, Klopp soon proved to be more adaptable from a tactical point of view than many expected.

That is not to say that he has moved away from preferring an aggressive pressing style when his side are out of possession but rather that he has adapted this part of his game model to suit not just the demands of the English game but the strengths and capabilities of his playing squad.

Before we start to look in more depth at the way that the pressing game at Liverpool has evolved over Klopp's tenure, and break down what this has looked like over the course of the

2019/20 season, we perhaps need to understand exactly what is meant by *gegenpressing*.

Whilst Klopp was in charge of Borussia Dortmund we saw the club begin to have success with a young team filled with players who had been recruited intelligently from a wide variety of interesting markets. The most important concept of the attacking game model for the German side was that they would attack quickly in transition as they looked to counter-attack through vertical passing movements. Initially, this meant that Dortmund would sit in a deep block defensively as they looked to invite the opposition to move forward in the attack before counter-attacking and taking advantage of any spaces that the opposition had left behind them. Gradually, however, this concept was joined with another in that when out of possession Dortmund would look to press aggressively against their opponent. This was especially true when Dortmund gave the ball away in the final third; these situations were pressed more aggressively than most as Klopp instructed his players to try to win the ball back as quickly as possible.

This style of the press had similarities, of course, to the way that Barcelona pressed when out of possession under Pep Guardiola. There was one key difference. Barcelona would commit one or at most two players to press and engage the ball carrier while the other players collapsed back into a more compact defensive block, but under Klopp we saw Dortmund flood the immediate area of the ball with pressing players. It was not uncommon to see up to four Dortmund players looking to put immediate pressure on the ball at the same time.

The reasoning behind this style of press is relatively simple. Klopp believed that winning the ball back so high up the field, as the opposition players were moving to transition from defensive positions to an attacking shape, gave his side a good chance of creating and scoring chances.

This was the first time that we started to see Klopp referring to the way that he wanted his players to press as being similar to a playmaker for the team. Indeed, when discussing the impact of *gegenpressing* in this manner in a post-match press conference, Klopp said, 'Think about the number of passes you have to make to get the player in the number 10 role into a position where he can make that genius pass. *Gegenpressing* lets you win the ball nearer to the goal. It's only one pass away from a really good opportunity. No playmaker in the world can be as good as a good *gegenpressing* situation, and that is why it is so important.'

So, we know that Klopp arrived in England as a huge proponent of *gegenpressing*. This incidentally is translated to English as counter-pressing with the central aim being that you press the opposition counter-attack before they can move into advanced areas of the pitch. But have Liverpool been a counter-pressing team throughout his reign at the club?

## Changes in PPDA of Liverpool from 2015/16 to 2019/20

| Club | Season | PPDA | League average |
|------|--------|------|----------------|
| Liverpool | 2015/16 | 7.610 | 9.610 |
| | 2016/17 | 8.200 | 10.770 |
| | 2017/18 | 9.510 | 11.660 |
| | 2018/19 | 10.080 | 11.870 |
| | 2019/20 | 9.100 | 11.670 |

**Figure 19**

*Figure 19* is a table that can help us begin to answer that question. We have used a metric known as PPDA to show the intensity of the press from Liverpool in every season under Klopp. PPDA stands for *passes per defensive action* and allows us to measure how many passes teams allow the opposition to have before they engage them in a defensive action. The lower the PPDA the more aggressive the press.

As we can see the average PPDA in Klopp's first season in charge, which also includes pressing numbers from the matches overseen by Brendan Rodgers, was the lowest we have seen at 7.61 PPDA and from there the PPDA has risen each year reaching 10.08 PPDA in the 2018/19 season. Interestingly, though, the number has again dropped in 2019/20 to 9.1.

While the PPDA has risen each year, however, it is worth noting that it always remains below the league average. The fact that we saw Liverpool's PPDA drop again this past season suggests that they have gone back to a more aggressive pressing structure.

While initially we saw Liverpool adopt a pressing style that was similar, if not identical to, that of Borussia Dortmund this has been adapted significantly to what we see today.

When the high press is triggered we see the front three for Liverpool be incredibly aggressive in engaging and closing down the ball carrier.

What is notable, however, is that whilst at Dortmund the pressing was intense but perhaps not always tactically intelligent, now at Liverpool the press is intelligent but also intense. When pressing the first line of the opposition build-up one player engages while another will move to press whilst also using his body position to prevent the sideways pass to escape the press. Beyond that we see Liverpool move to a man-to-man pressing structure that is designed to prevent the man in possession from having an easy way to play through the line of pressure.

We should note, however, that this form of high press is not the *only* pressing concept that we see from this Liverpool team and this is part of their genius out of possession. Whilst they do have the capacity to press and engage the ball high and to cut off passing lanes they are also comfortable when creating and triggering a series of pressing traps that force the opposition to play into areas of the field in which a press will be triggered to force a turnover.

One of the most notable differences that we see from the press of Liverpool in the 2019/20 season is that the forward players are now more passive than they have been in the past. The wide forwards tend to move to cut off passing lanes out to the full-backs while the central striker presses the goalkeeper or central defender. The press, however, is not triggered fully until the ball travels to the second line of the opposition, typically the midfield line, where the Liverpool midfield then becomes active in pressing and engaging the ball carrier while the front three join in to press from behind the ball. This form of press, with players moving from in front and from behind the ball, is designed to squeeze the man in possession and prevent the ball from being easily played away from the press. If the midfield line was the only form of pressure then the opposition could turn the ball back to their defensive unit to reset the ball and change the angle and point of attack. With the forward players moving from behind the ball, however, this escape option is taken away. The point of any pressing system, of course, is to force a turnover. If the pressing team cannot win the ball back from the initial player in possession then they hope that the player in question will be rushed into playing a poor pass that can be intercepted and turned over before they launch an attack in transition.

We do still see another form of counter-pressing from this Liverpool side as they move the ball through the thirds in possession. We tend to see them form a compact attacking shape with a lot of players positioned in a tight unit on the ball side of the field. While this is, of course, designed in an attacking sense to provide the capability to form overloads that will enable them to break through the defensive block of the opposition, there is a defensive function in this positioning as well. With a compact attacking unit, which includes the defenders playing high, we see Liverpool positioned perfectly to counter-press should the opposition win the ball back. Then this compact shape again transitions quickly into an attacking shape and the opposition can be overloaded as they struggle to move back to a defensive transition from an attacking one.

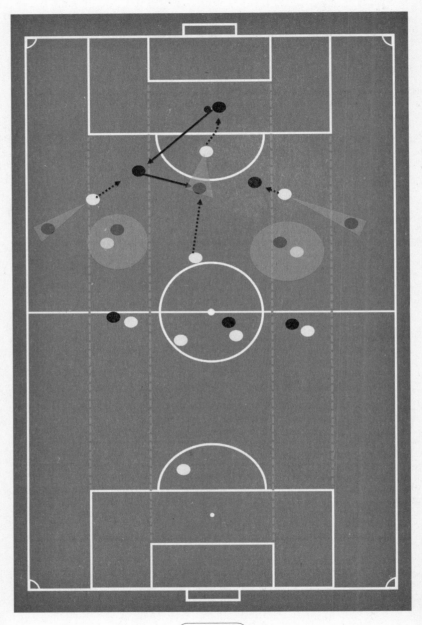

**Figure 20**

In *figure 20* we see an example of the typical pressing structure that we have seen from Liverpool over the course of the 2019/20 season. With the ball originally with the opposition goalkeeper only the striker, Roberto Firmino, moved to engage the ball. The two wide forwards are positioned between the central defenders and the full-backs of the opposition and as the ball is progressed to the central defender they maintain their distance and use their body shape to cut off the pass out to the full-backs.

There are, of course, differences in this style of play depending on who they are playing. Some central defenders are dangerous in possession of the ball, Virgil van Dijk for example, while others are less active when progressing the ball. Sitting off and not pressing some defenders is a better strategy than allowing the likes of Van Dijk the same space, for example.

Here, however, the opposition are able to access the pivot at the base of the midfield whilst first playing to the central defender. This movement is designed to bypass the first line of pressure from Liverpool and to give them a more advanced platform that they can play from. This, however, is a trap of sorts and when the ball is received by the pivot he is facing his own goal. The Liverpool '6' is then free from his position, where he has no direct opponent, to move to engage the ball from behind while Firmino does the same from behind the ball. These pressing movements combined with the fact that the wide forwards are still able to move to cut off the pass out to the wide areas make it very difficult for the opposition to safely play out of the press.

Liverpool show a definite preference for allowing the opposition to progress from the first to the second line in central areas. Wide spaces are more dangerous, despite the lack of space on the outside, while centrally Liverpool display a level of tactical understanding and intelligence that allow them to prevent the ball progression comfortably.

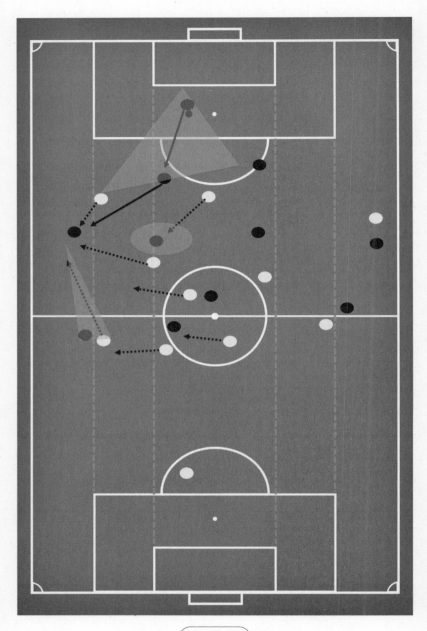

**Figure 21**

When the opposition is able to play out to the wide spaces as they progress the ball to the second line. We see a different form of pressing trigger that is in place to allow Liverpool to choke off any potential passing options.

We see this in *figure 21* as this time the ball is progressed out to the opposition right-back in the wide area. It is worth keeping in mind that in any given match even the best pressing structures can be played through. What we discuss are the concepts and tendencies that we see from Liverpool on a consistent basis.

This time the initial press has been beaten and the opposition have accessed the wide space. We have already discussed above the fact that this is something that Liverpool tend to try to avoid. What we can see, however, is that the position of the ball triggers a pressing movement that is even more difficult to bypass than the one that we saw above. As the opposition right-back collects the ball three Liverpool players move to engage the player: Sadio Mané, Andrew Robertson and Georginio Wijnaldum. These three players move to press the ball at different angles and the man in possession is put under extreme pressure. Given the fact that the player in possession is positioned right out on the touchline their range of movement and passing is limited. The ball forward is difficult due to the pressure from Robertson moving forward from left-back, the ball backwards is difficult because Mané is pressing from the left-forward slot and the pass into the middle is difficult because Wijnaldum is moving to engage. To make the pass into the central area even more difficult the entire defensive block for Liverpool has slid across to their left to negate the space that the opposition have in which to play.

With no easy way to play through the press the opposition player will either turn over possession or play a poor pass to try to find a way through the defensive block.

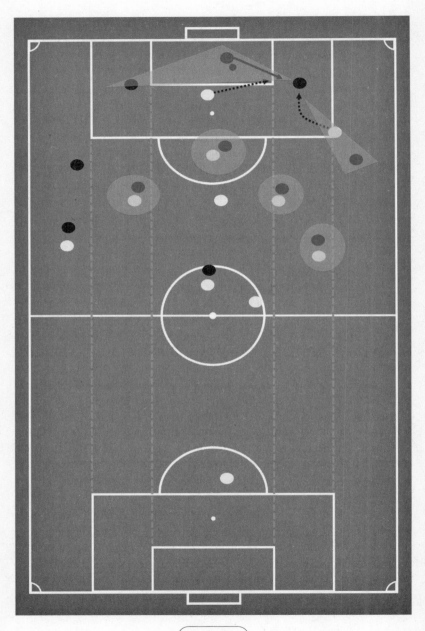

**Figure 22**

There are, of course, still situations in which Liverpool press the first line aggressively in order to try to force a turnover in possession. We see an example of this in *figure 22* as the opposition goalkeeper looks to find one of the two central defenders when both have dropped deep into the penalty area in order to receive and attempt to play progressively.

There is instant pressure put on the ball as Mohamed Salah presses from the right-forward position and Firmino presses from the centre. The key point in the movement from Firmino is that he curves his run as he moves to engage in order to keep his body between the ball and the opposition goalkeeper and second central defender. This seems like a small adjustment but it is crucial in preventing the ball from being played back to the goalkeeper or across to the other side to escape from the press.

Now, look again and we see the next four passing options (those closest to the man in possession of the ball) are all being marked man to man.

Once again the aim of the press is twofold, to either win the ball back high and progress to goal or to force the opposition player to do something rash and end up giving the ball back to Liverpool.

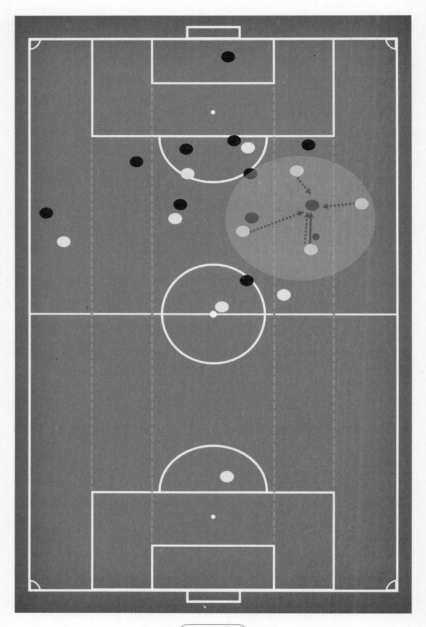

**Figure 23**

We also made mention earlier in the chapter that part of the effectiveness of the counter-pressing that we do still see from Liverpool comes in their ability to retain a compact shape both in and out of possession.

*Figure 23* shows this as Trent Alexander-Arnold gives the ball away with a simple vertical pass in the half-space. The opposition player had read the pass and shifted across to be in position to intercept and look to transition to the attack. The key, however, is that immediately there are four Liverpool players in position to counter-press to win the ball back. As Liverpool progress the ball through the thirds and enter the final third the entire structure moves as one with the central defenders tending to take positions as high up as the edge of the centre circle in the opposition half. This then allows the midfield line to squeeze higher towards the ball and provide connections to overload in possession and counter-press out of possession.

*Chapter 5*

# Functional midfield

The ability to progress the ball through the thirds of the pitch and to threaten your opponent's penalty area is key in football. Having the bulk of the possession and dominating in terms of pass completion statistics means nothing if the ball moves sideways or even backwards as opposed to going forward. Possession without penetration into the opposition half is almost meaningless. The way that top teams progress the ball changes depending on the way that their squad has been constructed. Take Manchester City, for example, where ball progression mainly moves through the half-spaces where the advanced central midfielders, David Silva and Kevin De Bruyne, are responsible for moving into the final third and creating opportunities to combine with attacking team-mates. The picture is different at another top side, Borussia Dortmund, where the progression of the ball comes through the central defenders who look to play vertical passes to the wide forwards who tend to drift more into the half-spaces, again, to receive the ball. There is no one way to progress the ball through the thirds and the most important thing is to have a clearly defined strategy in mind and to build your game model in possession around the way that you plan to progress the ball. This is an area in which we have seen a clear shift from Liverpool over the course of the 2019/20 season.

The decision to encourage Trent Alexander-Arnold to move into a more inverted position gives them more control in central areas and allows him to become more active in possession of the ball. On the opposite flank, the vertical runs of Andrew Robertson allow the ball to be progressed towards the final third through quick passing combinations to access the space that Robertson is moving into; that space, of course, tends to be vacated through the movement of Sadio Mané as he moves into the half-space on that side of the field. Once again then we see how important the half-spaces are in the progression of the ball.

While Liverpool have moved to use their full-backs as the key components in their ball progression and as the movements ahead of the ball are key in allowing these movements to occur, it is interesting to note that we have not discussed the midfield players at all.

This movement towards a more clearly defined set of mechanisms to allow for the ball to be progressed has left the midfield players behind; that does not, however, mean that the midfield players are not important parts of this Liverpool system. It is impossible to be as successful as Liverpool have been over the course of the last two seasons with three players whose roles are purely incidental and not important parts of the overall game model.

Before we break down why the midfield is still important, despite the lack of tangible output from this area, we should understand the players that we are discussing.

## Liverpool central midfielders 2019/20

| Team | Player | Age | Minutes played |
|------|--------|-----|----------------|
| Liverpool | G. Wijnaldum | 29 | 2,459 |
| | J. Henderson | 29 | 2,000 |
| | Fabinho | 26 | 1,565 |
| | A. Oxlade-Chamberlain | 26 | 1,174 |
| | J. Milner | 34 | 847 |
| | A. Lallana | 32 | 439 |
| | N. Keïta | 25 | 401 |
| | C. Jones | 19 | 24 |

**Figure 24**

In *figure 24* we see a table showing all of the players who have featured for Liverpool in the 2019/20 season in the centre of the midfield. This table has been ranked to show the players who featured most often at the top.

There are several takeaways from this table but the first is that there are three players who have featured on a regular basis. Georginio Wijnaldum leads the list, at the time of writing, with 2,459 minutes followed by Jordan Henderson with 2,000 minutes and Fabinho with 1,565 minutes. These three key players have provided the fulcrum of the Liverpool midfield over the course of the 2019/20 season. It is worth considering, however, the age profile of these three players; with both Wijnaldum and Henderson already aged 29, they are approaching the point where midfield players tend to start to regress. Fabinho, on the other hand, is 26 years old and at his peak. Given what we already know of the squad building favoured in recent seasons at Liverpool, signing players just before they enter their peak to ensure peak performance, it is likely that we will see both Wijnaldum, who has just a year left on his contract, and Henderson receive less playing time as we transition into the 2020/21 season. Interestingly, in terms of age profile their replacements are already in the squad with Alex Oxlade-Chamberlain, 26-years-old playing 1,174 minutes, and Naby Keïta, 26 years old playing 401 minutes, in place. Both have lost playing time over the course of the 2019/20 season due to injury issues and in Oxlade-Chamberlain's case these issues are recurring but both are highly regarded by the Liverpool coaching staff.

The thing about this potential shift in first-team minutes, though, is that this would see a complete change in the profile of the midfield. We have already seen in a previous chapter the importance of the '6' at the base of the midfield but we also have to consider the roles of the two other central midfielders from what has become the 'first-choice' midfield under Jürgen Klopp.

It is interesting to note that Henderson and Wijnaldum have very different playing profiles and this translates on the pitch.

The Dutch international Wijnaldum is an active defender but a lot of what he does on the pitch does not actually translate fully to any form of statistical or event data. He does engage with the press but not aggressively. Instead, Wijnaldum excels when positioning himself in such a way to block the passing lanes which might otherwise allow the opposition to progress the ball. In doing so he slows the attack of the opposition and allows team-mates who were involved in the attacking phase to recover their defensive position.

In possession, he also has a specific role to play, although not one that seems him directly involved in goalscoring all that often. We have already seen that the role of the '6' is extremely important to this Liverpool side but the position that Wijnaldum tends to play, as the left-sided central midfielder, is equally important. We tend to see Wijnaldum maintain if not the same line at least one that is similar to the '6' when Liverpool are in possession of the ball. He is a high-volume passer but not one that tends to progress the ball regularly. Instead, he will recycle possession and act almost as a pivot on his own as he takes the ball and shifts the angle of attack quickly and efficiently.

The role of Jordan Henderson is extremely different from that of Wijnaldum and not least because of the different movement patterns that we see from the English international. With the inverted movement of Alexander-Arnold into the half-space, we have already seen in earlier chapters that Henderson makes the movement to the outside that provides width. Indeed, a lot of what Henderson does in the attacking phase adds to the idea of chaos as a central concept in the Liverpool system. When Henderson first signed for Liverpool in 2011 he had played primarily as a box-to-box midfielder who was as active in the attacking phase as he was in the defensive. Somewhere along the way, Henderson was converted to a '6' at the base of the midfield and he filled this role for both Liverpool and England. By assigning Henderson a role in this position though, you are essentially limiting his effectiveness. He is a capable if not tremendous passer but his strength lies in his ability to make runs towards the edge of the penalty area which unbalances the defensive block of the opposition and creates space that team-mates can exploit. He displayed this continuously throughout the 2019/20 season with late runs into the penalty area that provided an option for team-mates to play the pass through the defensive line. This is equally true whether the starting point for those runs was from the right-hand side of the pitch or from the central areas.

In the defensive phase, the chaotic element of Henderson's game is even more evident. If Wijnaldum is passive, but effective, in the pressing game Henderson is anything but that. He presses and looks to dominate the game in those transitional moments when neither side can be said to have the ball completely under control.

By potentially replacing these two midfielders with Oxlade-Chamberlain and Keïta in the near future Liverpool would drastically alter the function of their midfield block. Both Oxlade-Chamberlain and Keïta are ball carriers and have strong outputs in terms of their progression of the ball. They are both active pressers out of possession and prefer to be proactive in winning the ball back from the opposition as quickly as possible. While none of these factors are necessarily negative they do represent the potential for Liverpool to fall back into the trap that led to the implementation of this more passive and functional midfield unit.

Having a more functional midfield block became essential for Liverpool following the issues they faced in the 2018/19 season. In this season we saw Liverpool come within inches of winning the Premier League title and despite beating Tottenham Hotspur to win the Champions League there remained a sense of disappointment in the season as a whole. Throughout the entirety of that season, Liverpool were a dominant force on the attacking side of the ball but in the defensive phase there were clear issues. One of these surrounded the lack of balance that they maintained while in possession of the ball. As they attacked and committed the full-backs into high positions the two advanced central midfielders would also move up to support the attack. This meant that when the attack broke down and the opposition regained possession they were able to attack quickly in the transition to take advantage of the spaces that Liverpool had left in their defensive third. By changing the roles and responsibilities of their midfielders Liverpool were looking to find a way to negate this defensive issue.

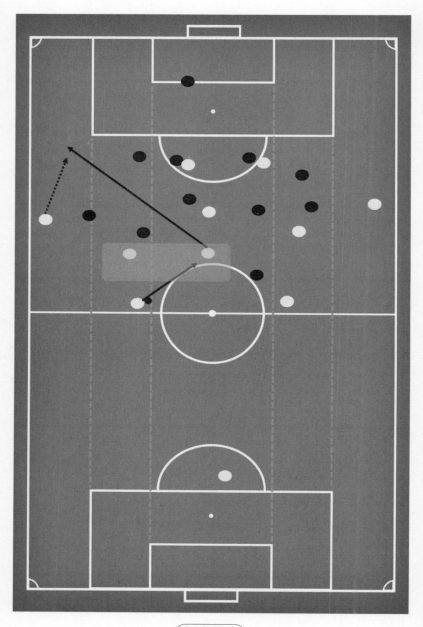

**Figure 25**

The different positional slots that we tend to see from the *first-choice* Liverpool midfield are interesting given how different they are.

To give an example of how they look and interact with one another we have provided an example from a game situation in *figure 25*. Wijnaldum and Fabinho are closely connected on the same line but Henderson has made that run that became so familiar out to the right-hand side.

The movement of the ball in this example was relatively simple with Van Dijk playing it into Fabinho who then accessed the space on the left-hand side where Robertson was moving into an advanced position from deep.

What is perhaps more interesting, however, is the balance in the system. Even though Henderson has moved outside, the inverted movement into the half-space from Alexander-Arnold provides balance alongside Fabinho and Wijnaldum. The occupation of space is also key with one player in each wide area and two players in each half-space. The rest of the structure for Liverpool is positioned centrally to take advantage of any opportunity that they may have to overload the centre of the opposition defensive block and break through on goal.

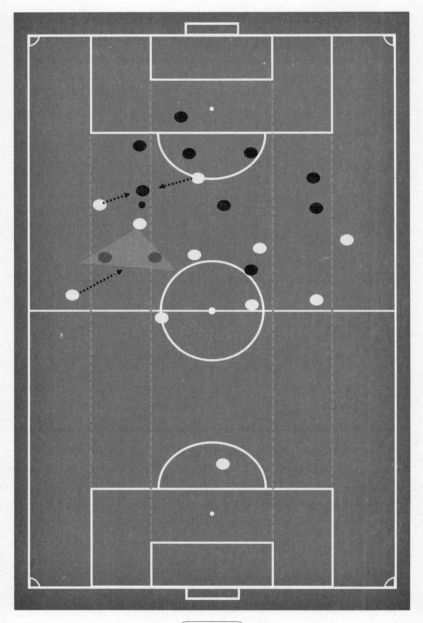

**Figure 26**

In *figure 26* we see an example of the defensive responsibilities that Wijnaldum has in delaying the attack and allowing the press to take place. As the opposition player in possession receives the ball Wijnaldum is actually the Liverpool player that is closest to him positionally. Now, the timing of the press becomes key. If Wijnaldum moves too quickly to engage the ball then the opponent in possession may be able to quickly shift the ball away from the Dutchman to access the space in behind.

Instead, we see Wijnaldum using his body position to essentially shield the passing lanes that the man in possession could use to find a team-mate behind the line of the Liverpool midfield. This positioning from Wijnaldum delays the pass from being made and allows two other Liverpool players to move to engage the ball and press the man in possession from different angles as they win back possession in the opposition half of the pitch.

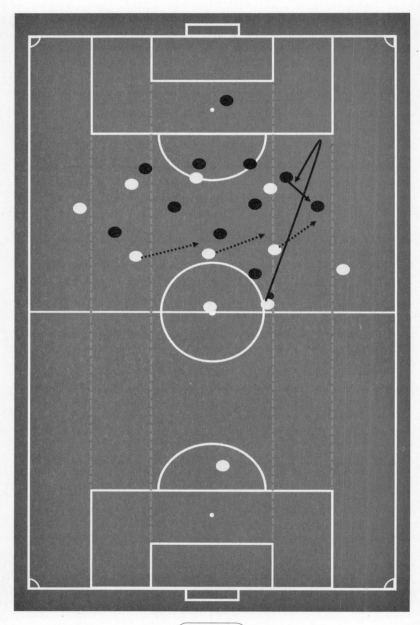

**Figure 27**

*Figure 27* shows an example of the way that the midfield unit works at the moment in which the ball is lost and they look to transition from attack to defence.

A direct pass is made forward as they try to find Mohamed Salah at the edge of the penalty area but the opposition recovers the ball and can launch a counter-attack. At this point, however, we see the midfield block slide across to close down the space that the opposition have to play into on that side of the pitch. Again, the key here is that the midfielders provide a block that will delay the progression of the ball for the opposition.

This movement of the midfield block is an important aspect of the passing structure that Liverpool use even if the players in question do not appear to be as active as others as they delay the pass forward and let other players press the ball from behind.

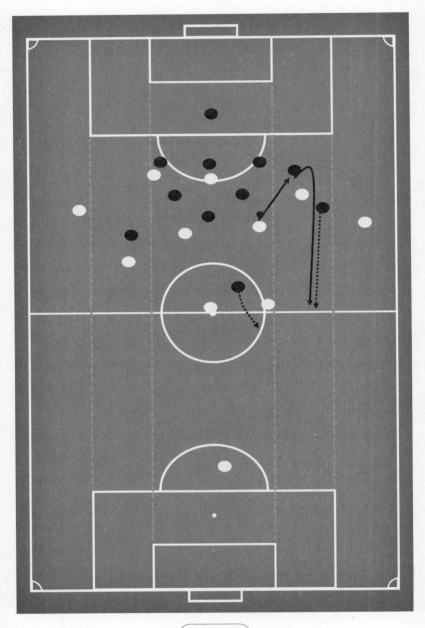

**Figure 28**

The final example for this chapter, *figure 28*, shows the importance of the functional midfield in the sustained defensive phase. While it is, of course, true that the first priority for Liverpool when out of possession is to press and win the ball back in order to create a goalscoring opportunity, there are, of course, going to be times when the opposition are able to have a more sustained period of possession.

In these situations, Liverpool are capable of forming a more compact defensive block to prevent the ball from being played into the penalty area. The midfield line of three, of course, is active in these situations as they primarily shield the two central defenders to prevent the ball from being played into the penalty area. On the left-hand side Sadio Mané comes back to support the defensive block but both Roberto Firmino and Mohamed Salah are positioned in higher areas to give a reference point should the ball be played forward.

The likes of Wijnaldum and Fabinho are perhaps more positionally sound and they shield the defence more effectively while Henderson is the player who tends to move out towards the ball in pressing movements more actively.

## Chapter 6
# The '9'

In the last chapter, we discussed the role of the functional midfield in this Liverpool game model. The three midfield players function in such a way that allows the more creative members of the Liverpool midfield to flourish. In another chapter, we discussed the role of the '6' or pivot player at the base of the midfield and that player's importance as a reference for the entire side in terms of positioning on the pitch. Now we get to the role of the second reference player who is crucial in enabling the rotations and movements of the attacking players around him, the Firmino role.

Why do we call this the Firmino role and not the '9' role in relation to the number generally given to the central striker in a 4-3-3 when roles are traditionally attached to the number of the player that we are discussing? The '6', the '8', the '10' and the '9' are all generally used in this sense. The difference, in this case, is that the profile of the position for Liverpool changes completely when Roberto Firmino is not in the side. There have been points in the 2019/20 season when the likes of Sadio Mané or Divock Origi have played as the central forwards in the 4-3-3.

What quickly became evident, however, is that despite Sadio Mané tending to play in central positions as he moves from the left-forward position the picture was very different when played as the '9' himself. Mané would constantly be looking to exploit the space behind the defensive line by playing on the shoulder of the defensive player and looking to use his pace to get on the end of through balls.

This is not surprising given the profile of the player. Mané relies on his pace and explosive movement when playing from outside to inside and he has the capacity to read the defensive structure of the opposition to take advantage of the spaces that appear in the defensive line. In this sense, Mané is one of the most dangerous attacking players in football. Playing as the '9', however, this space was harder to come by because there were no players who were in a position to drag defenders out of their slots to create space.

That is where the Firmino role comes in. Liverpool signed the Brazilian international from the German Bundesliga side Hoffenheim in 2015 but when they did so it was unclear whether they were signing a striker or an attacking midfield player. At Hoffenheim, we would generally see Firmino play from deeper positions from where he would move into advanced areas to support the striker and combine. Under Jürgen Klopp, however, we have seen Firmino firmly embedded in the '9' role from where his footballing intelligence provides much of the basis for the attacking structure of his side.

While we have seen other strikers, mainly Mané, played from the central positions their profiles are drastically different to that of Firmino. Where Mané favours movement beyond the defensive line and looks to stretch the height of the pitch we see Firmino look to drop into deeper areas of the pitch in order to create space for others.

This creation of space is one of the most important aspects of the game model of Liverpool when they are in possession and in the attacking phase. We have already discussed in previous chapters how the front three move and interact with one another and we have been clear that this interaction is a key component of the attacking game model. The movement from Firmino as he drops from the front line and into deeper areas is essential in creating opportunities for the wide forwards to move inside to occupy the central areas.

The movement from Firmino, to occupy deeper spaces, immediately causes problems for the opposition defensive block as he forces players to make difficult choices. Take the central defenders, for example; they have to choose whether to drop deep to follow Firmino into space or hold their position in the defensive line. If they drop deep then they create space that can be exploited by clever movement from Salah or Mané. If they retain their position in the defensive line then they are allowing Firmino to collect the ball in space and from this position he can turn in possession and create. The same choice is then forced on the central midfielder of the opposition. If they do recognise the movement from Firmino then do they drop deeper to shield the pass-through to his feet or do they stay in the slot and protect the structural integrity of the defensive block? Either choice exposes the defending team to a threat of space being exploited somewhere on the pitch.

When taking possession of the ball in these areas Firmino creates space for others but he also gives Liverpool an advanced platform from which the attack can play. This means that as the

Brazilian international takes possession of the ball he is able to receive and then control the tempo of the play. This advanced platform then allows all of the other aspects of the attacking structure to take place. We have already referenced the fact that the wide forwards then move inside to attack the space between the central defenders but this also allows the left-back to advance forward on the left-hand side and Jordan Henderson to pivot out to the right-hand side.

The beauty of these advanced platforms is that they are not limited to central positions but can be accessed from any position between the lines of the opposition midfield and defence. It is not uncommon to see Firmino coming into the half-space and dropping right back towards the halfway line in order to collect possession of the ball before linking with his team-mates in the wide spaces or acting as the pivot that allows a midfield player to move higher in order to provide more passing options.

We talk about the importance of progressive passing and having players who can break the lines of the opposition defensive structure with accurate forward passing and we have already discussed in a previous chapter the role that Trent Alexander-Arnold plays in moving the ball progressively. While these passes are incredibly important they are only relevant if they find a player who is positioned in these spaces between the line. Equally, if Firmino makes that run and there is no pass to break the lines then the run becomes almost meaningless.

This is a theory that was examined more fully by a German company called IMPECT as they began to collect what they called *packing* data. This data is designed to identify players on any team who are key in progressing the ball towards the opposition goal. If a defensive player, like Alexander-Arnold, makes a vertical pass that breaks the lines then the packing score is the total number of players that have been bypassed by that pass. The clever thing that IMPECT have done is to award those points not only to the player who plays the pass but to the player who receives the ball; they each receive an equal score. This data then allows us to identify who the best players are at finding these pockets of space between the lines as well as finding the players who are best at playing the passes that access these players. It should come as no surprise that Roberto Firmino scores extremely highly in the IMPECT data for passes received.

This role is one that is almost uniquely selfless. Most strikers consider it their 'job' on the pitch to access the penalty area and to finish chances but, for Liverpool, the bulk of the goal threat comes from the wide forwards while the full-backs are responsible for the progression of the ball into the final third and penalty area. The striker, therefore, in his Firmino role becomes almost a secondary threat in terms of goalscoring but he will play a key role in providing a creative threat for this Liverpool team.

When Firmino plays in this position one of the most important technical aspects that he brings to the team is his ability to receive the ball in tight areas of the pitch before manipulating it and keeping possession under pressure. This is something that is especially important when Liverpool are playing around the edge of the penalty area. We often see Liverpool progress the ball into the final third before looking to find the feet of Firmino with a driven pass. The Brazilian is capable of instant control and when he receives the ball in these areas and he is extremely press resistant, this means that he remains calm under pressure and is able to hold off the opponent trying to engage him to win the ball back. When the ball is played into Firmino in these areas we have grown familiar to his tricks and flicks as he tries to find a route through the final defensive line and into the penalty area. He also displays his creativity when waiting for team-mates to make forward runs that break the defensive line. These runs then allow Firmino to play the ball into the penalty area for a chance on goal.

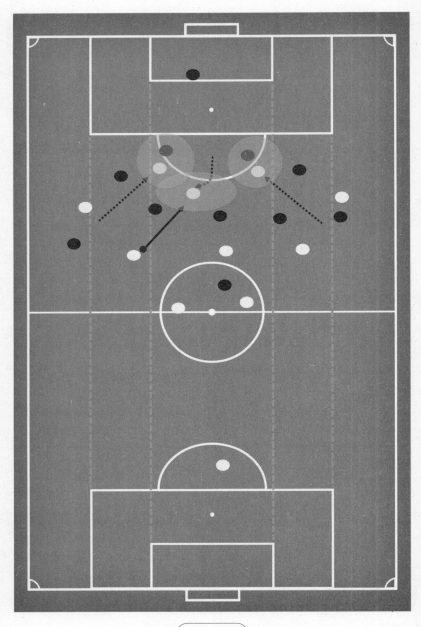

**Figure 29**

When we talk of the importance of Firmino dropping deep to access space in the final third and the way that this creates the opportunity for the wide forwards to come inside we are, in fact, only telling half of the story. The movement into deep positions does create the space for the likes of Salah and Mané to come inside but their movement into central areas is key in making sure that the space for Firmino is maintained.

We see this clearly in *figure 29* where Firmino has dropped into the '10' space. We talked earlier in the chapter about the fact that these movements forced the opposition players to make choices that impact the available space for Liverpool. In this example, however, we can clearly see that the movement from the wide forwards to come inside has essentially taken this choice away completely. Each of the two central defenders is now man to man with a Liverpool attacker and if they were to move out to engage Firmino as he takes possession of the ball then they would leave one of the most dangerous players in football free on the edge of the penalty area.

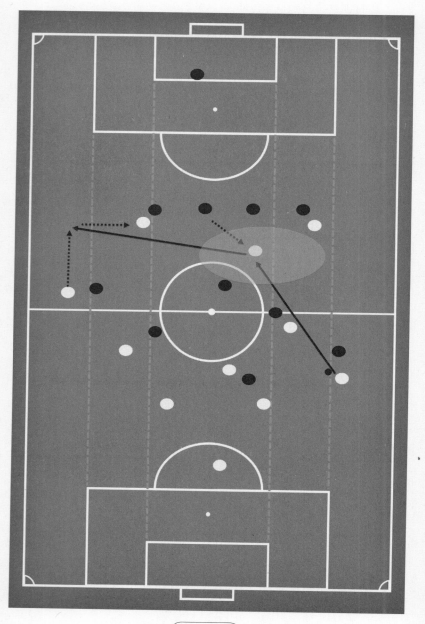

**Figure 30**

*Figure 30* sees a slightly different situation but again it is Firmino who is playing as the '9' and again he drops deep on the ball side of the pitch. It is this movement that provides the key to dragging defensive players towards the ball and opening space elsewhere on the pitch. As Firmino drops into this space he is left free by the central defenders who choose to maintain their defensive position. This is, of course, helped in part by the movement of the wide forwards who have already shifted infield. If one of the central defenders now moves out to follow Firmino then space is created in the defensive line for the ball to be played through for one of Mané or Salah to attack at pace.

This example gives a perfect insight into the creation in the opposition half of advanced platforms from which Liverpool attack. As the ball progresses from right-back to find Firmino there are six opposition players that are effectively taken out of the game completely. While those players can, of course, recover their position they will be trying to do so whilst running back towards their own goal.

Here, though, as Firmino takes possession he immediately has the time and space to receive and turn towards the opposition box. Now, as Mané has moved inside he has dragged the opposition right-back inside with him and this has created the opportunity for the left-back for Liverpool to advance into a high line. As Firmino turns, Andy Robertson is already moving ahead of the opposition midfielder and Firmino has the range of passing needed to access the diagonal pass into space.

From this position, with the opposition playing a relatively high defensive line we see that with one simple switch of play Liverpool are able to access the space to the side of the defensive line and the run of Robertson takes him comfortably beyond the defensive block. From this position, the defensive line is now having to recover back towards its own goal and the pace of the likes of Mané and Salah can be deadly.

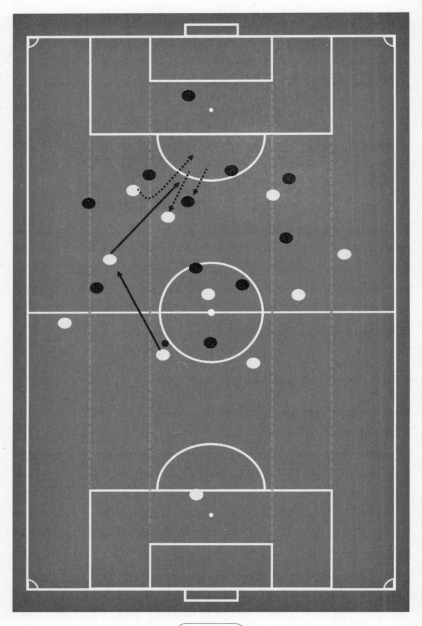

**Figure 31**

It is also important to note the effect that these deep movements from the '9' in this Liverpool system has when one of the defenders is pulled out of position. In *figure 31* we see Firmino dropping deep again, and again he moves towards the ball side of the field in order to create space. It is interesting to note at this point that different strikers will position themselves in different slots on the field. A striker who likes to use pace to penetrate towards the defensive line might pull off towards the far side to find space. Firmino, however, moves towards the ball in order to provide the link between the midfield and the attack.

Now, as Firmino drops deeper the right-sided central defender chooses to shadow him and he leaves a gap in the defensive line. This in a single snapshot is the beauty of the kinds of movement that Firmino makes when playing as the '9'. If the defender does not track the run of Firmino then the Brazilian creates a platform in the final third. If he does choose to track the run, as we see in this example, then a hole is created between the right-back and the left-sided central defender.

We see the ball progress from Virgil van Dijk in the defensive line forward to Georginio Wijnaldum and immediately the ball is then progressed into the space that has been created by the movement of Firmino. This pass through the defensive line allows Mané to accelerate away from the full-back into space in the defensive line. This led to an easy chance on goal.

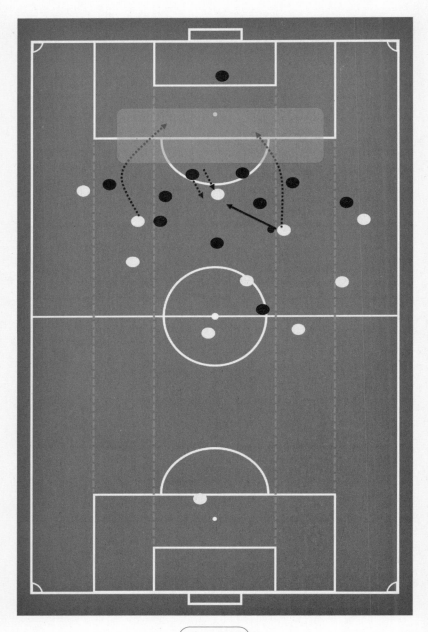

**Figure 32**

*Figure 32* shows another example when the defender chooses to follow Firmino as he drops off the furthest line. In the final third we see the Liverpool players have complete trust in Firmino's ability to receive the ball under pressure and hold defenders off. When the ball is played forward into the feet of Firmino he is press resistant and the other Liverpool players move forward immediately to support the ball.

With Salah in possession of the ball in front of the defensive line Firmino again moves towards the ball to give an option. The defensive player is following Firmino to prevent the Brazilian from turning but as soon as that pass is played into Firmino's feet we see both Salah and Mané immediately making vertical runs beyond the defensive line. As Firmino takes possession of the ball in this area and with a defender close behind him we see the Brazilian twisting and turning to lose the defender before finding the through ball to the highlighted space behind the defensive line.

These vertical runs are generally made by Mané and Salah but Robertson on the left-hand side also stretches beyond the defensive line whenever Firmino collects the ball in these areas.

These positions are so incredibly fundamental to the way that Liverpool look to play the game because the midfield is so functional. The ball is progressed towards the final third and from this position, the attacking movement flows and revolves around Firmino.

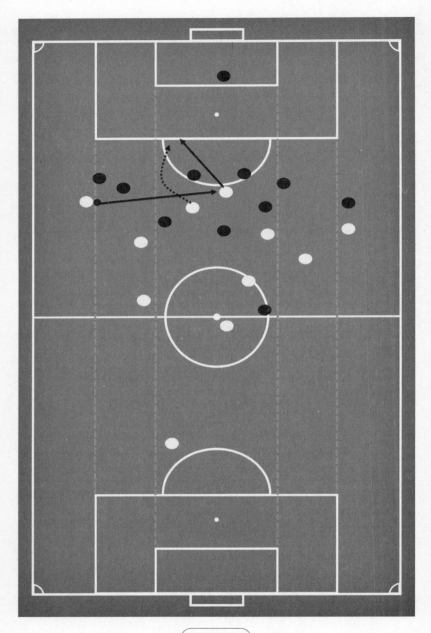

**Figure 33**

It is, of course, important to note that just because Firmino can drop into the '10' space it doesn't mean that he always does. As Liverpool advance and progress into the final third, we do from time to time find Firmino maintaining his position in the defensive line. We see an example of this in *figure 33* with the Brazilian positioned just in front of the opposition defensive line.

In these moments we again see the importance of the close control and press resistance of Firmino in this role. As the ball is moved laterally from Robertson, who has moved into a high position on the outside, Firmino receives the ball and immediately Liverpool have a central platform from which they can attack. This is the kind of position in which it is incredibly important that the striker has the technical ability to receive the ball in these spaces and then look to interplay. Here, as the ball is played into Firmino there is an immediate vertical run from Mané who starts from a deeper space and then breaks through into the penalty area.

The important thing here is that Firmino is able to receive the ball on one foot before then flicking the ball forward with his opposite foot through the defensive line.

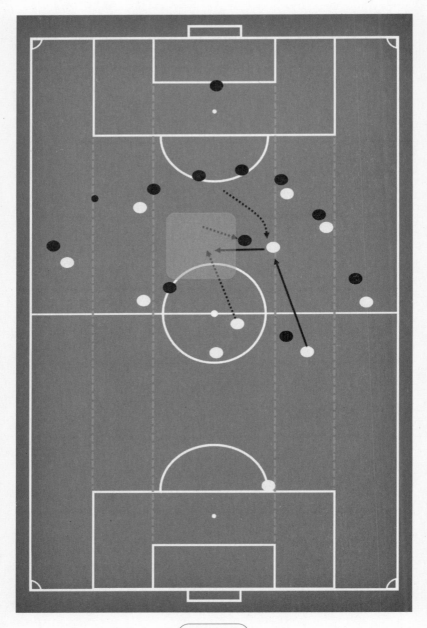

**Figure 34**

The vast majority of the work that the '9' does in this Liverpool system does, of course, take place in the final third. But there are points in which Firmino comes far deeper in order to affect the play and help progress the ball for his side.

We see an example of this in *figure 34* as Firmino drops back towards the halfway line, in order to both create space for a team-mate and allow the ball to be progressed. With Joël Matip in possession, he plays a vertical pass as Firmino comes towards the ball to receive in space. In doing so he moves past the opposition midfielder and immediately he forces that player to follow and break out of his defensive slot.

When Firmino then takes possession of the ball with the midfielder looking to press we see Jordan Henderson, who was playing as the '6' at the base of the midfield, as he then moves vertically into that space that has been vacated by the player who has followed Firmino deep.

The ability to pull defensive players out of their position in these areas is a key part of the system of play that Jürgen Klopp has put in place as it creates opportunities for players to attack spaces from wide or deep. This allows Liverpool to break through the opposition defensive block.

## Chapter 7

# False wingers

In footballing terms, we do not have to go too far back in time to find a point at which the tactical profile of the game was far more linear and simple. Full-backs were expected to stay deep and defend, strikers led the line and did not interact with the midfield and wide players stayed wide and looked to dribble past their opponent before crossing the ball into the box.

Over the last 10–15 years, however, there has been a significant development in how these roles and players interact with one another. Some would argue that football has become too tactical and those people would covet a return to a simpler time when coaches did not have the capacity to affect the game as much as they do now from a tactical perspective.

Indeed, if we break down the individual components of this Liverpool side, especially when they are in possession of the ball, then we see that almost every 'traditional' role has been altered in some way to fit a more cohesive tactical pattern. The key to this Liverpool system is that all of the individual components work together to create something that is greater than the sum of their parts. We have already discussed many of these components in earlier chapters and looked individually at the role of the central defenders and the full-backs in terms of progressing the ball as well as considering how the striker works in a selfless manner in order to create spaces for his team-mates. The final one of these components that we need to look to break down is arguably the most important, the role of the wide forwards.

Liverpool's first-choice players in this area are clearly defined with the Senegalese international Sadio Mané playing from the left-hand side and the Egyptian international Mohamed Salah playing from the right. The signings of these two players represent the strength of the scouting and recruitment departments currently in place at Liverpool with neither seen as a 'sure thing' when they joined the club in 2016 and 2017 respectively. Indeed, Mohamed Salah was considered by many as having already *failed* in the Premier League following a spell with Chelsea in which he was not given the playing time that young players need to continue their development. Many also thought that the club overpaid for Mané when they paid their Premier League rivals a reported £34m for his services.

These signings, however, represent proof, in hindsight at least, that Liverpool were already acutely aware of the system that they wanted to put in place and the importance of having players who fit this profile.

The idea of having wide players who cut inside, almost as inside forwards, is nothing new. One of the most famous examples of a player making these movements is the former Dutch international Arjen Robben who, during his time at Bayern Munich, made this movement something of an art. Taking the ball out on the right-hand side we would see Robben consistently shape as if to go outside the defender before quickly moving inside where he was able to use his left foot to strike the ball, often from distance, at goal. Indeed, it became a regular feature of the game at the top level for coaches to play wide players on the 'opposite side'; this means that left-footed players would play on the right-hand side and right-footed players would play on the right-hand side. This meant that when these players picked up possession of the ball in the attacking phase for their teams their natural inclination was to come inside to attack in the half-spaces. From here, on their stronger foot, more of the pitch is immediately opened up.

There is another reason that this tendency to prefer inverted wide players became more prevalent as it created the space and opportunity for full-backs, who were becoming more attacking orientated; by having wide forwards who displayed clear tendencies to move inside, the opposition full-back was also drawn inside to cover the movement. This created the space for the full-back to move high and stretch the width of the defensive block. This type of movement was extremely effective against sides who would look to defend in a deep and compact defensive block as the inverted movement created opportunities for quick overloads in central areas while the vertical movement of the full-backs provided the opportunity to play wide and around the defensive block in order to get behind the defensive line to create opportunities on goal.

This was a relatively common pattern of play that we started to see from teams on a regular basis but Liverpool took the concept further and refined it to the point that the wide forwards were functioning more as traditional strikers who position themselves across the width of the opposition penalty area. What this essentially meant is that the roles of players in the final third were switched. Traditionally, wide players created chances and strikers looked to be in a position to finish them. For Liverpool, the opposite is largely true. While the striker, normally Firmino, drops deeper and looks to create space and goalscoring opportunities the wide players move centrally to occupy the defensive line and try to create goalscoring opportunities. These movements are even more pronounced when we start to consider where these opportunities come from. The vast majority of shots, and indeed goals, that both Mané and Salah take are within the width of the penalty area and even inside the penalty area. Contrast this to what we know of the typical inverted winger and again we will reference Arjen Robben, while he made the movements from the outside to cut in and run at the opposition defensive line but in the vast majority of these attacking movements we would then see Robben shoot from well outside the penalty area at angles that carried a lower chance of resulting in a goal. To frame this reference a little more we have to accept that Robben was a *scorer of great goals* as opposed to being a *great scorer of goals* and his highlight reel is full of shots from these areas being bent around the goalkeeper from outside the penalty area. The positions in which Mané and Salah find themselves are far more conducive to the creation of goalscoring opportunities that carry a high expected goals value. Expected goals is a metric that is designed to value the chance of a shot from each area of the pitch resulting in a goal. The models that calculate this metric are built to reference thousands of goalscoring opportunities and gradually each shot is assigned a value from 0.01 to 1.00 based on the likelihood that they will result in goals. The shots that we have described from Robben, for example, would carry a low percentage chance of resulting in a goal. Shots from the positions that Mané and Salah find themselves in have a much higher percentage chance of ending in a goal. Given what we know of the use of advanced metrics and algorithms from Liverpool in their recruitment strategy it should come as no surprise that they would first of all recruit players, like Salah and

Mané, who can take shots from high-value areas and of course that they would then play these players in a structure that makes the most of these positive traits.

While so far we have referenced both Mané and Salah as though they perform similar roles it is worth noting that they actually have very different player profiles and that these profiles complement one another incredibly well.

Firstly, though, we should explain the player profiles a little more to show how these are essential elements to consider when building your squad. Player profiles refer to the tendencies that a player has combined with their personalities and how they interact with one another. While we are not in a position to accurately comment on the personalities we can discuss the tendencies that make up these profiles. Take Mané and Firmino, for example; while Firmino tends to play centrally and Mané tends to play from the left side there was a point in the 2019/20 season in which Firmino was unavailable and so Mané played as the central striker. It was in these moments that we saw how important player profiles can be. As discussed in the last chapter, Firmino is selfless in his movements to drop off of the front line into pockets of space and this is important in allowing the wide forwards to take up these central positions. That tendency from the Brazilian to drop deep is a part of his profile; he does not look to make many runs in behind the defensive line and instead tends to drop off and link play. Contrast that to the games in which we saw Mané utilised from a central attacking position. He constantly looked to make the run off the shoulder of the defenders to access the space behind the defensive line and this alters the attacking structure of Liverpool and the spaces that are available for other players.

So, if we go back to Mané then we already have a key piece of information that makes up his profile. He likes to use his pace to make runs behind the defensive line. This is something that tends to be far more effective when the starting point for his run is deeper. From the half-space his ability to make sharp and aggressive vertical runs can be devastating to the opposition defensive block. Mané displays a clear preference for passes to be played into space and to receive the ball when facing goal.

We can contrast this to Salah who, despite also having excellent pace, has a preference for receiving the ball into feet. He occupies the same kind of positions as Mané but when receiving the ball he likes to initiate contact with the defensive player before using his physical strength to hold off or roll the defender in order to create a path into the penalty area. Another of Salah's strengths is that he possesses the ability to create shots with little or no warning. Normally players are fairly pronounced with their movements when preparing to shoot; their stance changes and they go through a definite shooting motion. Salah is able to generate great power in his shots with very little backlift and as such when he turns the opponent inside the penalty area he can shoot without warning.

Now consider how these two player profiles interact with one another, and with Firmino. We already know that Firmino drops into the '10' space but now we can start to build in more information. Salah will play centrally and look to receive the ball with his back to goal on the right-hand side or central area of the penalty area. Mané, on the other hand, will always look to move higher to take advantage of spaces that might open up beyond the defensive line.

Now consider how hard it is to defend against a Liverpool team who have the capacity to play on so many different lines and in so many different ways.

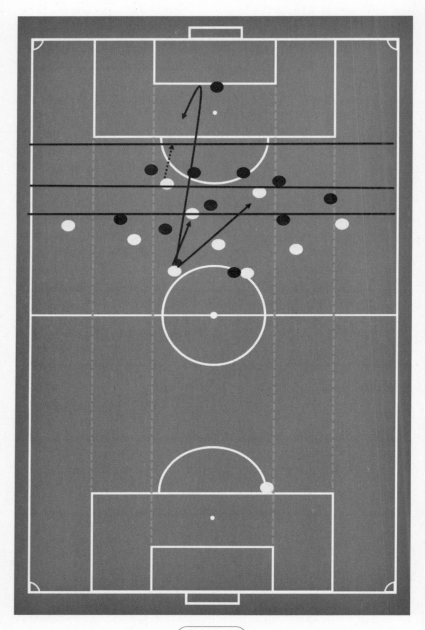

**Figure 35**

The first thing that we should note when considering the positioning of the wide forwards in the attacking phase is the way that they interact with the central striker in order to take up what amount to separate lines in the final third.

We have an example of this in *figure 35* as Liverpool are in possession of the ball at the edge of the final third with little or no direct pressure on the ball. Virgil van Dijk has possession of the ball on the first line and the opposition are unable to place him under reasonable pressure. We have already discussed in an early chapter the importance of the central defenders and their role in progressing the ball when they have space on the ball. The two wide forwards have inverted and are positioned in the central space. This is a mark of just how far these players move inside; they do not just drift into the half-space as many wide forwards do.

Now, consider the different tendencies of the three players that traditionally play in these positions for Liverpool – the wide forwards and the central striker. We know that Firmino drops deep and looks to receive. Salah also looks to receive the ball to feet but instead of dropping deep, he is comfortable isolating against a single defensive player so that he can get into 1v1 opportunities. Mané, on the other hand, is pulling into space between defensive players and looking to stretch beyond the defensive line.

All of these different tendencies then operate as one; with Van Dijk in possession he is able to reach any of these three lines.

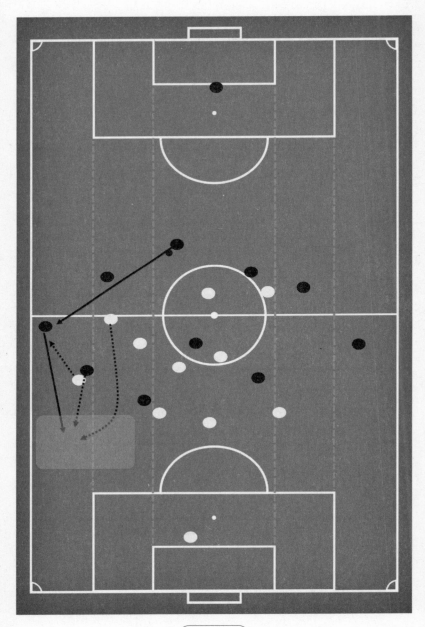

**Figure 36**

While discussing the tendencies of the wide forwards for Liverpool it is easy to concentrate only on the established attacking phase but their performances out of possession are equally important. In *figure 36* we see an example of this as the opposition are looking to build down the right-hand side of the pitch. As the central defender, who is initially in possession of the ball, plays the ball out to the full-back we see Andy Robertson move out to engage with the man in possession and in doing so an opposition player suddenly finds himself in space. This player would normally then be passed over to the near-side central defender or central midfielder but instead we see Mané moving at speed from a high position to provide cover.

As the man in possession on the opposition right-hand side then turns the ball around the corner the opposition think that they are in a strong attacking position. Mané, however, works diligently off the ball and is able to get into position to challenge for the ball and start an attacking transition of his own.

It should be noted that whilst this defensive work is not unusual for Mané on his side of the field the same cannot be said for Salah over on the right. The Egyptian forward will press the ball in the initial moments of transition but when the opposition crosses the halfway line he stops and retains a high position in order to be in place for the attacking transition when Liverpool win back possession.

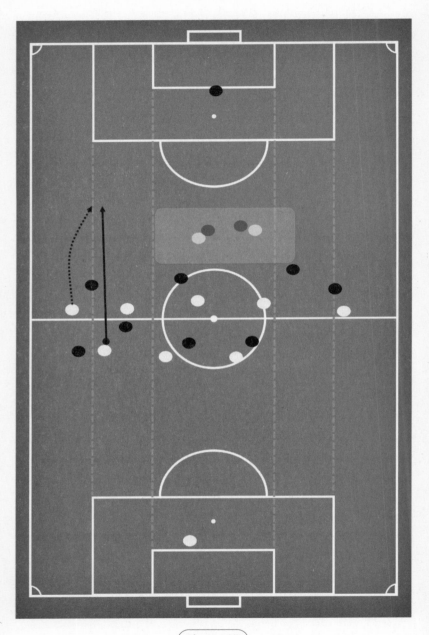

**Figure 37**

From these moments of transition, the pace of Mané tends to be integral in turning the opposition and accessing the space that they have left in behind as they move into attacking positions.

We see an example of this in action in *figure 37* with Liverpool winning back the ball initially with Robertson in the left-back position. You can see that Salah and Firmino are positioned centrally and their presence has pinned the opposition central defenders into a deep position and this means that they are unable to move out to defend the pass into space.

Robertson plays a relatively simple vertical pass and immediately Mané is able to make a curved run to the outside of the defensive player who is high and isolated against the Senegalese forward.

This simple piece of play with a straight pass and a run that moves outside the defender is enough to completely unbalance the opposition defensive transition.

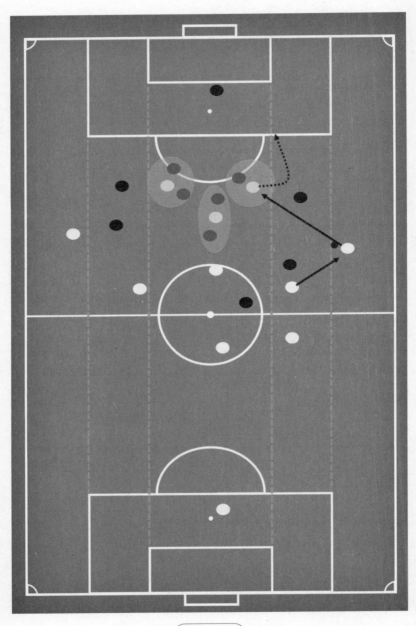

**Figure 38**

The movements of the wide forwards are key in occupying and pinning defensive players in place, as we can see in *figure 38*.

We have already seen the importance of the different tendencies that the front three players for Liverpool have. These tendencies are part of the individual player profiles that create such difficulties for opposition defences. We already know that Mané prefers passes into space that allow him to access using his pace and the timing of his runs. In this example, however, we see the kind of positions that Salah tends to take up in order to access the penalty area. Both Firmino and Mané are positioned in such a way to attract the attention of two defensive players and this plays into the hands of Salah.

With four defensive players already effectively taken out of the picture, we see Salah showing for the ball and demanding a pass played into feet. As the ball is fed into the Egyptian forward he is able to take possession isolated in a 1v1 situation. Salah is excellent when using his low centre of gravity to turn and twist and beat defenders who have got too tight in order to challenge for the ball. We see this in action in this example as Salah receives the ball and then allows the defender to get close before rolling to the outside to access the penalty area. From this area, the Egyptian forward finished calmly across the front of the goalkeeper.

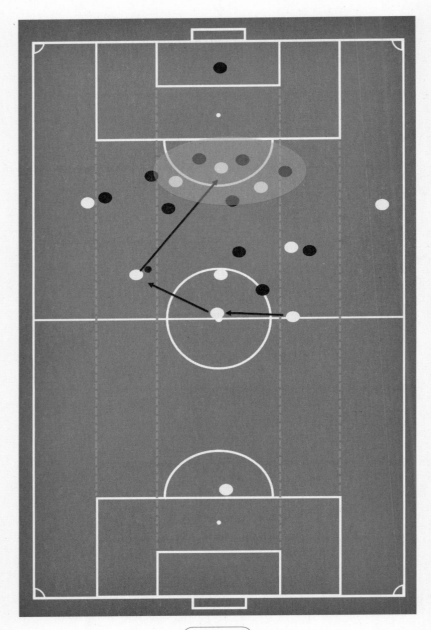

**Figure 39**

When Liverpool force their opposition back into deeper positions there is a tendency for the two wide forwards to take up central positions alongside the lone striker. This movement inside is something that we have touched upon extensively already but its importance cannot be overstated.

Take the situation that we see in *figure 39*, for example, with the ball being circulated along the Liverpool defensive line from Matip to Van Dijk and then on to Wijnaldum. Now, look at the positioning of the two wide forwards combined with the central striker. They are all in the central area and this time the striker has not dropped deep. Instead, they have created an immediate overload against the opposition in the central areas of the pitch. As the ball is played forward into this zone the wide forwards are positioned in the lanes between the central defenders and the full-backs. This allows them to attack these spaces vertically as the striker takes possession of the ball; in these situations Liverpool are at their explosive best.

## Chapter 8
# Virgil van Dijk

The career progression of the Dutch central defender Virgil van Dijk is a fascinating one to look back on and carries a multitude of lessons for youngsters that want to forge a career in football. To start with Van Dijk is possibly one of the few world-class players in football today whose future was anything but clear when he was a young player. Indeed, his career path to this point further highlights this uncertainty as he appears to have taken incremental steps to get to the point that he is at today.

Virgil van Dijk began his footballing career with Willem II in the Netherlands but despite progressing through each tier of their youth system he was never offered a professional contract at the club. Eventually, Van Dijk was contacted by the directors of Willem II and advised that Groningen were interested in his services and that the club were happy to let him go. Even then, however, the young defender had to overcome doubts. Some coaches at Groningen criticised Van Dijk for switching off too often and becoming casual with his approach to defending. Even then he possessed such physical capacity that he was able to recover his position if he had allowed the opposition striker to have too much space. This physical advantage, however, was likely to diminish as Van Dijk progressed towards the first team. Gradually, though, Van Dijk did establish himself as a first-team regular at the centre of the defence and there was a great deal of speculation that he would make the next natural step in his career progression, with a move to one of the traditional Dutch giants of Ajax, PSV Eindhoven and Feyenoord.

While each of those three clubs were interested and had scouted Van Dijk extensively an offer was never made. In 2013 a concrete bid for Van Dijk was made by the Scottish club Celtic. Even then, though, Van Dijk held out hope that he could still take the next step in his career in the Netherlands. With talks over a move to Celtic at an advanced stage contact was again made with Ajax but their sporting director, Marc Overmars, declined to make an offer, a decision that he would surely come to regret. That left the way open for Celtic to seal what would be a bargain deal with Van Dijk moving to Glasgow for a fee reported to be in the region of £2.6m.

At Celtic, we saw Van Dijk exposed to a completely different style of football. While Groningen were a mid-tier side who were rarely expected to completely dominate the game, the opposite was true of Celtic. In Glasgow, the young defender was exposed to a different style of football and one in which, in possession, the central defenders were seen as key components in ball progression, in the same way that they are today with Liverpool. Van Dijk also had to become accustomed to defending when isolated and running back towards his own goal. Because Celtic were so dominant from a possession standpoint it was normal to see their central defenders positioned in the opposition half as they were attacking. This compression of space led to the opposition looking to attack quickly through direct play over the head of the Celtic defenders. As, such Van Dijk became accustomed to using his pace to defend when isolated 1v1 against opposition attacking players.

It was at Celtic that another aspect of Van Dijk's game began to emerge as he was recognised as a leader both on and off the pitch. He exuded calm on the pitch but was very vocal and would regularly adjust the positioning of his team-mates if he felt they were becoming slack. Gone was the casual approach that had followed him throughout the early stages of his career. Even with the standard of play in Scotland being recognised as generally poor, the performances of Van Dijk soon saw droves of scouts crossing the border from England to watch the Dutch defender in action. In what was becoming a common feature when it came to discussions around Van Dijk, however, some talent evaluators were still unconvinced, citing the relative lack of competition that Celtic faced domestically and feeling that they were still unsure as to whether Van Dijk could make the step up in level to the Premier League.

Luckily for Van Dijk, and quite possibly for Liverpool, one club was not deterred and in 2015 Southampton paid a reported £13m to sign Van Dijk and bring him to the Premier League. Although the profit that Celtic had made on trading Van Dijk was already impressive the Scottish club also inserted a clause in the detail that entitled them to a percentage of any future transfer deal; in retrospect this looks like an inspired move from the Scottish club.

Now, at Southampton, we began to see Van Dijk turn into the player that we see today at Liverpool. The step up in the competition did not overwhelm Van Dijk and, instead, he raised his game to more than deal with the forwards that he came up against in the Premier League. The issue for Southampton, however, was that despite their strong performances with Van Dijk they were still a middle-tier club and this left them exposed to some of the so-called 'super clubs' in England becoming interested in their new star defender. Eventually, this interest came to a head with Jürgen Klopp making it clear to the

*Sadio Mané of Liverpool getting past Billy Gilmour during the FA Cup match between Chelsea and Liverpool at Stamford Bridge on Tuesday, 3 March 2020.*

*Liverpool manager Jürgen Klopp in characteristic pose at Anfield.*

*Home-grown right-back Trent Alexander-Arnold, a first-team regular and full international by the age of 19.*

*Virgil van Dijk at Carrow Road, Norwich on 15 February 2020.*

*Fabinho celebrates a rare goal in Liverpool colours.*

*Midfielder and captain Jordan Henderson surveys the scene at Carrow Road.*

*Naby Keita is challenged by Genk's Junya Ito during the UEFA Champions League match at the Luminus Arena, Genk.*

*Mohamed Salah – prolific for both Liverpool and Egypt.*

*Roberto Firmino's role is key to Klopp's style of attacking play at Liverpool.*

*Jürgen Klopp celebrates after the penalty shoot-out win against Chelsea during the UEFA Super Cup Final at Besiktas Park, Istanbul.*

*Philip Billing of Bournemouth is tackled by Trent Alexander-Arnold at Anfield.*

*Liverpool's Mohamed Salah (centre) celebrates scoring another Liverpool goal.*

*Sadio Mané has become a key member of the Liverpool team since his transfer from Southampton in June 2016.*

*Sadio Mané of Liverpool shoots and scores a goal to make it 0-1 during the Premier League match between Norwich City and Liverpool at Carrow Road, Norwich on 15 February 2020.*

Liverpool hierarchy that not only was Van Dijk his top target to play in defence, but he should also be considered his only target.

This triggered a period of negotiations which stretched the relationship between the two clubs but eventually ended with an agreement announced in December 2017 that would see Van Dijk move to Liverpool at the end of the 2017/18 season for a fee of £75m, a huge profit for Southampton.

When you view the career of Van Dijk through the lens of his path to Anfield then you begin to understand the environment that has shaped the defender that we see at Liverpool today. Having come through periods of self-doubt at Willem II and then at Groningen and had to battle those that doubted his ability at Groningen and then at Celtic it should come as no surprise that Van Dijk is as confident and self-assured as he is.

Playing as the left-sided central defender in this Liverpool system we now see all of the tactical and technical knowledge that Van Dijk has accrued through his career clearly. When defending in deeper positions, as he learnt at Groningen and to a lesser extent at Southampton, Van Dijk understands how to manipulate and control space in a defensive sense. He has excellent range given his pace and the length of his reach and, as such, strikers struggle to find effective space in which they can receive the ball. When Liverpool are in possession he is confident in using the ball in possession and he always looks for the progressive passes that will break the lines of the opposition defensive structure. Indeed, at the time of writing in the 2019/20 season, Van Dijk is averaging 9.11 passes to the final third per 90 minutes and 10.43 progressive passes per 90. He is also comfortable defending within this high defensive line and he is averaging 8.61 possession-adjusted interceptions per 90 minutes.

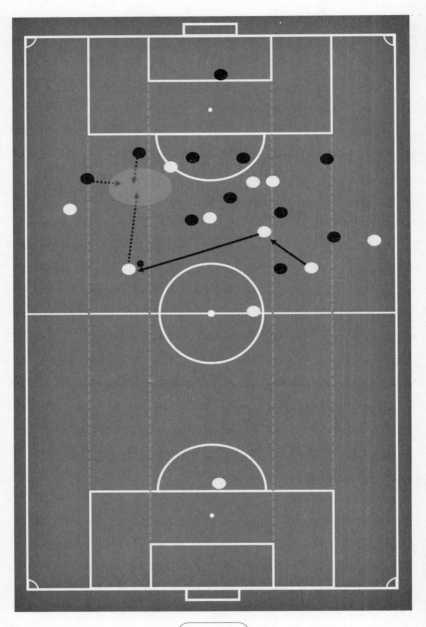

**Figure 40**

For a team like Liverpool, who enjoy the majority of the possession against any team that they play against, it is essential that their central defenders are comfortable in possession of the ball. We see an example of how Van Dijk is with the ball at his feet in *figure 40.*

The opposition are initially compact on the ball side of the field but, as we can see, Van Dijk is already completely free in the half-space on the opposite side of the pitch.

Liverpool simply work the ball across to the Dutch central defender through a simple passing combination. As soon as Van Dijk receives the ball in this position his first thought is to drive forward at the opposition defensive block. We have to recognise, of course, that as the ball is played across, the bulk of the opposition's defensive structure will look to pivot across to close down the vertical passing options that are open to Van Dijk. The Dutch international, however, does not wait for this shift and he carries the ball forward immediately. This movement of the central defender towards the defensive line of the opposition forces two players to move out of their positional slots to close Van Dijk down.

This movement towards the ball to engage and press leaves space behind that can be exploited by the movement of Robertson, from left-back, and Mané from the left of the attack.

If Van Dijk was not comfortable carrying the ball forward in this manner and simply looked to sit on the ball and look for a passing option then the opposition players could have retained their defensive shape and space would never have been exploited.

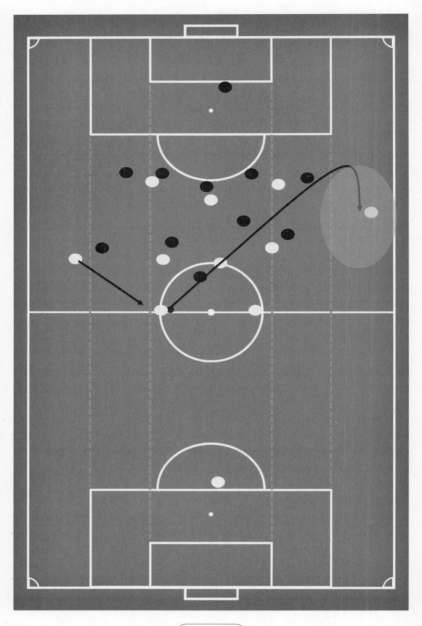

**Figure 41**

As well as being comfortable when moving forward with the ball and forcing opposition defenders to engage, Van Dijk also possesses the vision and passing range to access all areas of the pitch as we see in *figure 41*.

The opposition are set in a compact and effective defensive block as Liverpool have possession through Robertson in the left-back slot. The opposition are well set and they have players in position to press and engage the ball. Robertson plays a simple pass to Van Dijk in an effort to relieve pressure and quickly change the angle of the attack. As the Dutch defender takes possession of the ball the vertical passing options are both poorly positioned, too close to the ball, and covered by an opposition player. Instead, Van Dijk has the capability of receiving the ball on one foot before opening out his body to the other side and then hitting a high diagonal pass that accesses the wide space where Trent Alexander-Arnold looks to have pulled into a free area.

Consider then what we know of Virgil van Dijk in possession. Not only can he spread the play and quickly change the angle of the attack but he can take the ball and drive vertically in possession to engage the opposition defenders. As a progressive force then, Van Dijk is not a player that the opposition can afford to leave in space in possession of the ball.

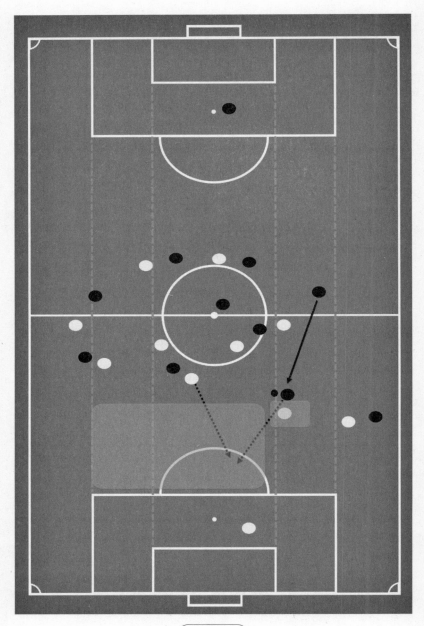

**Figure 42**

We also, of course, have to consider the capacity of Van Dijk to perform in the defensive phase. This is a situation from a match in the 2019/20 season against Spurs and we have highlighted the key moment in *figure 42*. As Spurs transitioned in the attacking phase they had the ball in the right half-space but Liverpool still looked to have control. That was until the defender covering the man in possession lost his footing and suddenly the man in possession was through on goal.

It is in situations like these, however, that we begin to see the kind of defensive dominance that Van Dijk brings to the team. The Dutch defender is immediately thrown into a 2v1 situation with the man in possession heading to goal and the player behind Van Dijk moving to support. Such is the incredible defensive capacity of Van Dijk that he is able to close down the ball whilst keeping the supporting player in his cover shadow and as the Spurs player moves into the penalty area we see Van Dijk in position to engage and win the challenge before launching an attack in transition for his team.

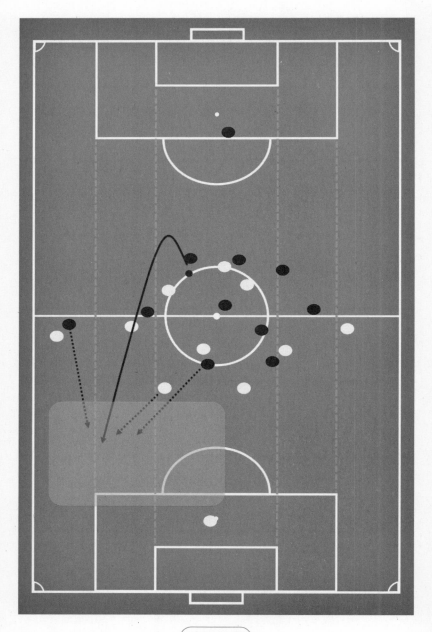

**Figure 43**

Virgil van Dijk is so powerful in the defensive phase that he controls large areas of the field, even when they are behind him and between the defensive line and the goal. He is comfortable defending in transition whether pulled out into wide positions or remaining central and cutting passing lanes or supporting defensive team-mates.

In *figure 43* we see an example of Van Dijk having to defend when running back towards his own goal and against multiple opponents.

The opposition have won possession of the ball with their central defenders and despite the counter-pressing movement from the central striker and the right-sided forward they are able to get a quick pass away. We have already discussed in previous chapters the fact that given the tendency of Liverpool to move into advanced areas with a high defensive line in possession, one of their weak points is the amount of space behind the defenders. Here we see the opposition looking to access this space quickly with two runners looking to move into the zone that the ball drops in. Unfortunately for the forward players, however, Van Dijk is extremely quick and he moves back where, despite being isolated against two attacking players, he has the capacity to get to the ball first before playing out of trouble.

The ability of Van Dijk to defend in these types of situations when the opposition suddenly have an attacking overload is one of the key reasons that Liverpool are able to allow their left-back to take up such advanced positions. Without Van Dijk, if the likes of Dejan Lovren were in the side, then the picture changes and Liverpool have to adjust their defensive system accordingly. With Van Dijk, they are able to access the full range of their attacking options.

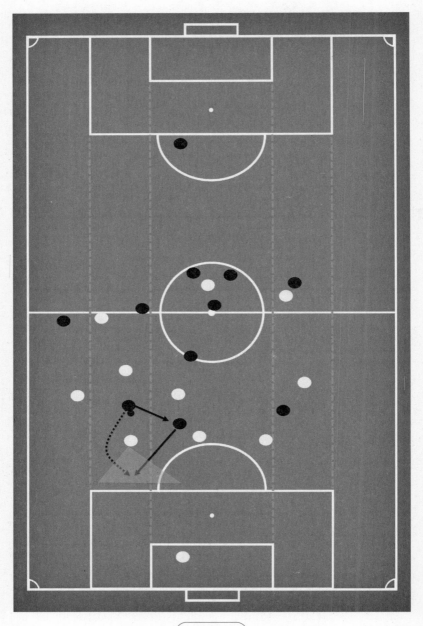

**Figure 44**

This ability that Van Dijk has to control space in the defensive phase is equally important when Liverpool are in a deep defensive block. The concept of having defenders that are capable of controlling space defensively is incredibly important because it allows defensive players to be isolated 1v1 against opponents and this, in turn, makes it harder for the opposition to create overload situations.

In *figure 44* we see a situation where the opposition have been able to build an attack into the final third and the ball carrier is positioned just ahead of Van Dijk. There is a supporting player positioned centrally, although he is technically covered by the second central defender.

The pass is played diagonally into the feet of the supporting player and he immediately tries to access the space behind Van Dijk with a layoff. As the initial attacking player looks to complete the attacking movement with a run around Van Dijk to access this space, however, he finds the Dutch defender positioned perfectly to deny the space.

Van Dijk possesses an innate sense of positioning with the ability to angle his body perfectly to cover passing options while also maintaining the balance needed to defend against the opposition attacking players should they take possession of the ball and try to run at the Dutch defender.

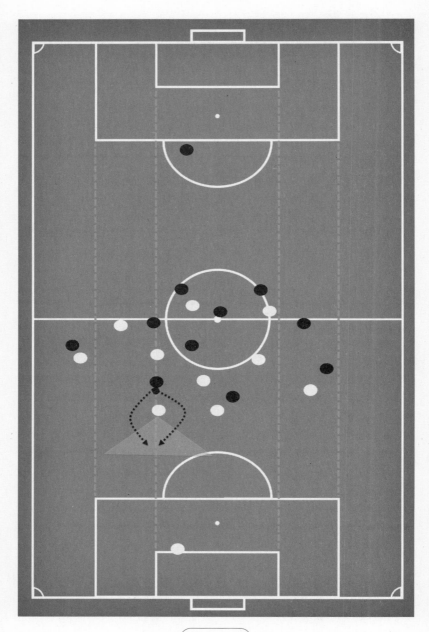

**Figure 45**

We see a clear example of this balance and ability to defend when isolated in *figure 45* with an opposition forward in possession and once again positioned just ahead of the Dutch defender. The second central defender is unable to provide effective cover because of the position of the second striker.

Most defensive players have a tendency to be more comfortable defending on one side or the other. For the most part, this is on the defenders 'strong' side. So if the defender is left-footed they are more comfortable if the attacker attacks down the left side and the opposite is true for right-footed players.

Van Dijk is one of the most complete defenders in world football because of his ability to defend just as effectively whether attacked on his left or on his right. In this example, the forward tried to drive inside Van Dijk thinking that he was less defensively strong on that side. Van Dijk simply opened out his body and shifted across to win the ball without even having to go to ground.

## Chapter 9

# Jordan Henderson

It says a lot about the overall quality of this Liverpool side that the player who is perhaps least secure in his position in the side is the club captain, Jordan Henderson. This is not to say, however, that Henderson is not a valued member of the side but rather that his role is one that is largely functional and not creative.

It is a measure of the mental resilience of Henderson that he is still viewed as such an important member of the Liverpool squad as he has long been criticised for his performances in a Liverpool shirt and for his perceived limitations. What is interesting, though, is that these limitations were largely caused by previous coaches using Henderson in positions and roles that did not suit his strengths or his player profile. The signing of Fabinho, to play as the '6', allowed Henderson to move into a more advanced midfield position and his tactical flexibility and athleticism in these positions has proved to be extremely important for Liverpool.

Jordan Henderson made his Premier League debut as an 18-year-old with his hometown club Sunderland. He enjoyed a brief spell on loan at Coventry City but soon returned to the North East to become a key figure in the Sunderland first team. His athleticism was quickly on show as he figured out on the right-hand side of midfield where, despite lacking the pace normally associated with a winger, his industry and ability to play an active role in both the attacking and defensive phases of the game stood out. Gradually we saw Henderson make more of an impact in a central role as Sunderland experienced injuries to their more experienced players in that position. From this point on Henderson never looked back and he was rewarded with a five-year contract as Sunderland looked to tie him down to a long-term deal.

This contract was, however, not enough to keep Henderson at the club and in 2011 he made the move to Liverpool for a fee believed to be around £18m. This transfer represented a significant investment from the Anfield club at a time at which their recruitment strategy was just starting to become more analytically focussed. Liverpool are currently owned by Fenway Sports Group (FSG) and they secured the deal to take control of the club in 2010. FSG were already owners of the Boston Red Sox, the storied baseball franchise, and they had become convinced by the Moneyball strategy that had allowed Billy Beane and the Oakland Athletics to consistently perform above their means against much larger franchises, including the Red Sox.

Moneyball, in a baseball sense, was a relatively simple concept. The Athletics began to evaluate players using advanced metrics that the majority of baseball organisations were not paying attention to. In doing so they were able to identify players who were undervalued and could be acquired for far less than the players who performed better in more established metrics.

Those behind the FSG groups had already begun to implement the same kind of strategies at the Red Sox and they were increasingly convinced that the same principles could be applied to football with Liverpool. In order to put this in place, FSG appointed the Frenchman Damien Comolli in a new role, director of football strategy. In this position, Comolli, who had previously had roles with Arsenal, Spurs and Saint-Etienne was responsible for the recruitment strategy at the club.

This led to a group of signings that had mixed success, to say the least, at Anfield; the winter transfer window saw two new strikers arrive, Luis Suarez, from Ajax, and Andy Carroll, from Newcastle. At the end of that season, attention was turned to players who Comolli felt could have an impact in creating chances for these new strikers and three were identified and brought into the club. Charlie Adam arrived from Blackpool with a reputation for delivering dangerous balls into the box from set plays while both Stewart Downing and Jordan Henderson were also signed due to their impressive output in terms of creating chances for team-mates.

Of the five players mentioned only Suarez, eventually sold to Barcelona for a significant profit, and Henderson can be considered a success but the role that Henderson ended up playing was anything but a creative one. In the end, Comolli left Liverpool by mutual consent in 2012 amidst criticism of recruitment decisions that were perceived to have been failures. This entire episode was an interesting precursor to the data-driven recruitment approach that we see as an integral part of the way that this current Liverpool side has been built. It is a credit to FSG that they stuck with their belief that data could be key in player recruitment despite this initial setback.

Back, though, to Jordan Henderson, and so far during his Liverpool career he has played under three different coaches and his role has changed slightly with each. Initially, under Kenny Dalglish, we saw Henderson used sparingly as he tried to adapt to the difference in environment having moved from Sunderland to Liverpool. Next came Brendan Rodgers and the first change of role as Henderson became used most often as the '6' in the pivot position at the base of the three-man midfield. While Henderson was capable of playing in this role it certainly did not play to his strengths. Rodgers preferred the '6' to be relatively static and to provide a function that would allow the ball to be recycled through the midfield as a part of the possession-heavy system that Rodgers preferred. This role prevented Henderson from making the kind of line-breaking runs through the midfield and into the final third that had become a key factor of his game. His style of passing, usually safe and not progressive, was suited to this role but fans soon became frustrated by what they saw as an unwillingness to pass the ball forward into the final third.

This role was continued when Jürgen Klopp replaced Rodgers as coach but there was an obvious disconnect between what the German coach expected from his '6' and what Henderson could provide. The signing of Fabinho in 2018 appeared to be a negative development for Henderson with many believing that this would see the amount of first-team minutes given to Henderson fall significantly. Instead, we saw Henderson released back into the role that suits him best as he played as one of the two '8's in the Liverpool system. The mobility and power that made Henderson so successful at Sunderland was suddenly a key ingredient for Liverpool as he moved from the inside to the outside in order to provide width on the right-hand side while Trent Alexander-Arnold moved inside to occupy the half-space more readily. That is not to say, however, that this positional flexibility is all that Henderson brings to Liverpool. He is an aggressive presser of the ball who is key for Liverpool when they are counter-pressing out of possession but he still gets involved heavily in the build-up when Liverpool are in possession of the ball. At the time of writing Henderson was averaging 69.44 passes per 90 minutes, which is the third most amongst this Liverpool side behind only Virgil van Dijk and Joe Gomez. It is worth noting as well that Henderson is averaging the most passes per game into the final third of the pitch in this Liverpool side with 11.97 per 90 minutes. This goes to show that the lack of progressive passing under Brendan Rodgers was likely to have been due to tactical instruction rather than a lack of ability or will to play progressively.

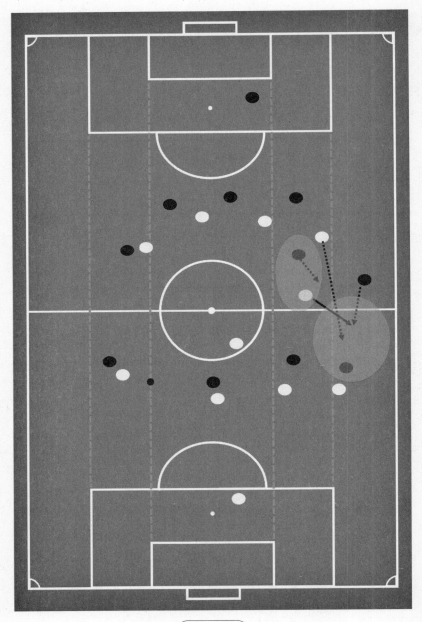

**Figure 46**

Jordan Henderson is one of the most underrated members of this Liverpool side and his ability to perform effectively in both phases of the game are extremely important in this tactical system. Out of possession, his athleticism and work rate see him equally comfortable whether defending back towards his own goal or pressing the ball to deny the opposition the opportunity to play forward.

In *figure 46* we see an example of this athleticism out of possession as Henderson works to recover his position. This particular example was from a match in the 2019/20 season against Norwich City. Liverpool had been in the attacking phase but the attack was broken down before a chance could be created. The Norwich player who took possession of the ball was able to advance forward and he was engaged by Trent Alexander-Arnold in the half-space. The challenge slowed the attacking transition down but the ball still broke to the Norwich player on the outside and suddenly Norwich were moving forward in a position where they would be able to create an overload on the ball side of the pitch.

That was, however, until Henderson made a defensive run from well behind the ball to move into position to not only block the run of the man in possession but to win the ball back and launch an attacking transition of their own. Jordan Henderson is capable of transitioning quickly from one phase to another quickly and while the rest of the functional midfield of Fabinho and Wijnaldum carry out more screening roles.

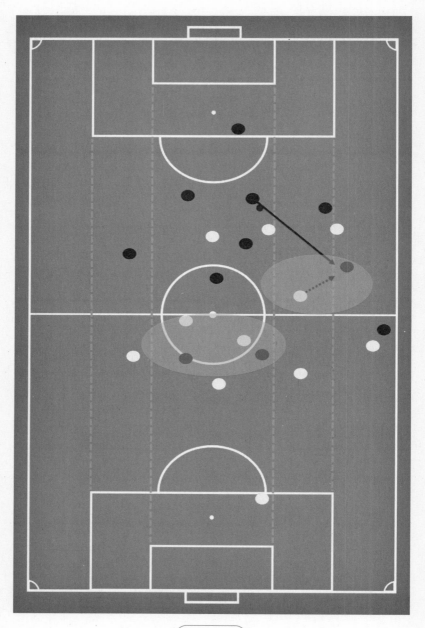

Figure 47

This time, in *figure 47*, we see a situation where Jordan Henderson provides a key role in pressing out towards the ball in order to prevent a quick transition from the opposition. Once again the other two midfielders take up a set position behind the ball but they do not move to join the press. This is one of the key differences in pressing structures between this Liverpool side and the Borussia Dortmund of Klopp – the press is far more measured.

As Henderson moves to press the ball he closes the space around the ball and prevents the opportunity to play either wide or in a more direct way to the front line. This press, however, is not purely designed to win the ball back but to act as an effective delaying tactic. This allows the front players to collapse back on to the ball from behind and it is at this point that the ball is won back by Liverpool. This form of counter-press from Henderson is largely situational but his ability to press and then recover if the ball is played beyond is extremely effective.

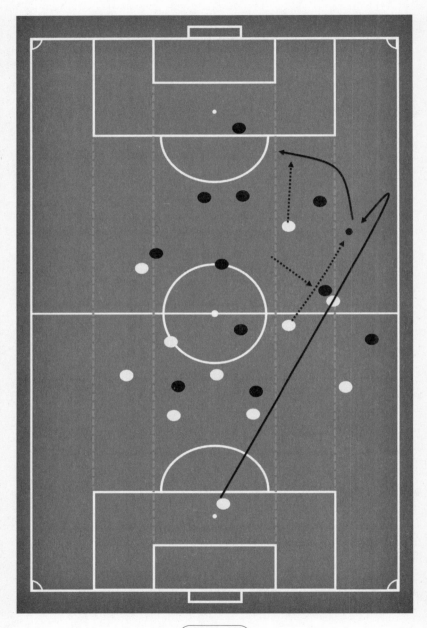

Figure 48

This athleticism is equally effective for Liverpool when they are in possession of the ball. His ability to cover ground at speed adds a definite sense of dynamism to the Liverpool attack. We see this in *figure 48* as Liverpool quickly transition in the attacking phase.

The initial pass comes forward from the goalkeeper who plays a direct ball into the opposition half of the field. Roberto Firmino had dropped off towards the midfield and this movement has pulled an opposition defender back with him.

The Brazilian is not successful in winning the ball but it rolls loose out to the right-hand side. Henderson makes a decisive movement out to the right-hand side of the field and he collects the loose ball.

It is, of course, not enough to just be able to move out to collect possession in this wide space; the player also has to be able to make the pass in behind the defensive line. The initial movement of Firmino was effective in dragging a defensive player out of the slot and, as such, there is a space between the defensive players. Mohamed Salah is positioned between two players on the defensive line and he is immediately looking to make a vertical run to break the line of the opposition and access the space behind the defensive line. Jordan Henderson has the quality on the ball to be able to take possession and bend the pass around the defender into the path of Salah for a chance on goal.

Henderson effectively controls a large part of the pitch because of his mobility and willingness to work both in and out of possession.

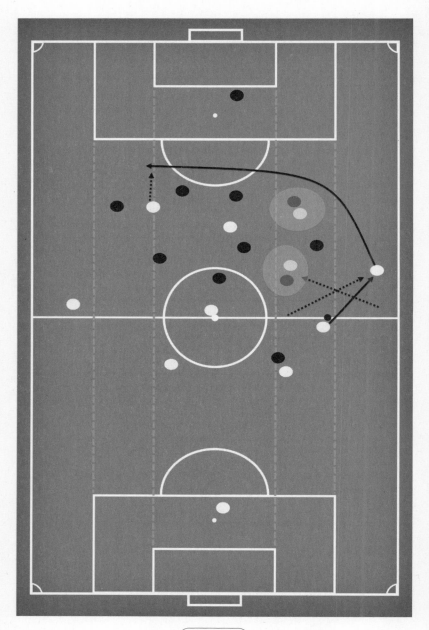

**Figure 49**

In *figure 49* we see another example of Henderson being able to position himself in a free area to control a section of the pitch all on his own.

The space is created through a simple rotation that we see regularly from Liverpool as Alexander-Arnold moves into his now standard position in the half-space. As he does so he drags the defensive player inside with him and Henderson makes the run outside to provide the width and prevent the central space from becoming overloaded. This is a mechanism that we have described at some depth so far in this book but it is so important in the way that Liverpool stretch the opposition defensive block to create space that their attacking players can access.

In this example, Henderson collects possession of the ball and displays his passing range to access the key space behind the defensive line. The pass is curled into the space between the defensive line and the goalkeeper into space where Mané is positioned between two defensive players and in position to run on to the ball.

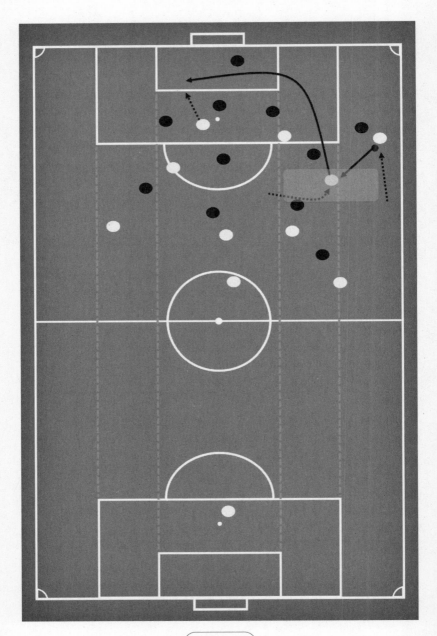

**Figure 50**

Another key position that we see Henderson occupy in the Liverpool attacking structure is a supporting one when he pulls out to the angle of the penalty area behind the ball. In *figure 50* we have captured this moment from a match against Southampton. The ball had initially been played outside to Alexander-Arnold on the right-hand side and the young English full-back had advanced wide into space instead of moving inside as he tended to do over the course of the last season. As Alexander-Arnold moves into a more advanced position, his run is tracked by a defensive player and the cross into the penalty area is made far more difficult.

This is where we see Henderson move over to support the ball, but at an angle, he is able to receive the ball and then we see what has become something of a trademark for the English midfielder as he curls his foot around the ball first time and loops a cross towards the far post.

These supporting runs are further supplemented by late bursts into the opposition penalty area when the attacking phase is slowed down. Henderson displays a variety of tools in order to access the penalty area whether from wide spaces or more centrally in support of passes being played into the penalty area.

## Chapter 10

# Fabinho

The Liverpool of the 2019/20 season is full of world-class players who have the capacity to win games almost on their own. From Alisson Becker in goal to Virgil van Dijk in defence all the way up to the front three of Sadio Mané, Mohamed Salah and Roberto Firmino there are a string of players who have been recruited by the club and who represent the kind of intelligent transfers that have provided the bedrock of the success that Liverpool have been experiencing for the past two seasons. Arguably, however, none of these five players is the signing that provided the platform for this success; instead, that honour goes to the Brazilian international midfielder Fabio Henrique Tavares, known as Fabinho. While the defensive and attacking contributions of the other five players are of course incredibly important, Fabinho is the only player who can be seen to have just as important an impact on Liverpool whether they are in or out of possession. His positioning, pressing and reading of the game are all standout defensive qualities that allow Liverpool to push into more advanced positions when they are attacking. If the opposition wins the ball back and transitions to the attack then Fabinho has the capacity to provide cover centrally or in the wide areas. In the attacking phase as well he is important in providing the control and reference point centrally while the other attacking players rotate and move around him in the final third. This flexibility and ability to impact the game in both the attack and in the defence is incredibly impressive, even more so when we consider that up until just a couple of seasons ago Fabinho was unhappy at being made to play in the centre of the midfield as he favoured playing as a right-back.

Fabinho was originally in the youth system at Fluminense but he did not make a senior appearance before taking the familiar route to Europe for Brazilians as he signed for the Portuguese side Rio Ave in 2012 on a long-term deal, or what was thought to be a long-term deal. Instead, after a matter of weeks in Portugal, the young Brazilian was loaned to Spanish giants Real Madrid on a one-year deal. This is not to say that Fabinho was necessarily ready to make the move to the top level; instead, he was signed to play at right-back for the Real Madrid B team that plays in the lower leagues of Spanish football. Still, it was a clear sign of the potential that the young defender was thought to possess. That season saw Fabinho given his debut in the Real Madrid first team under the Portuguese coach Jose Mourinho. However, the young Brazilian never made any more appearances at the first-team level and he returned to Rio Ave at the end of that season. There were signs that Real Madrid wanted to take Fabinho again the following season but they never counted on one of the top clubs in Europe in terms of talent identification making a concrete offer for the player. So, instead of a move back to Spain, we saw Fabinho move to France to join AS Monaco on a two-year loan deal before signing for the club on a permanent deal in 2015. At this point, Fabinho was ready for first-team exposure in a top-five European league and he quickly became an important player for Monaco. At this point, however, we saw Fabinho moved to a different position at the base of the midfield. If we consider what we know about Fabinho today it is easy to see what made him such an effective right-back. He has both pace and power and a long stride that allows him to cover ground quickly both when moving forward and when recovering his position in the defensive transition. Indeed there were early comparisons to the former Brazilian international right-back Maicon due to similarities in their playing style. At Monaco, however, the coaching staff believed that those physical traits combined with a high football IQ and an excellent positional sense could translate very effectively to the defensive midfield role at the club. Initially, Fabinho was unhappy with the move, believing that it would impact his chances of breaking through to the Brazil squad on a regular basis and missing what he thought was his best position. Indeed, when discussing a contract with Monaco the Brazilian reportedly asked his agent to explore the possibility of building in a clause that would force the French club to play him at right-back. Ultimately this idea did not come to fruition and, instead, Fabinho played in the defensive midfield role and even at times as a central defender in France for the Monaco side that eventually made it through to the Champions League semi-final in the 2016/17 season.

It is a common feature of football that transfers between big clubs are long drawn-out processes that tend to be played out in the media. This was not, however, the case when Liverpool announced in May 2018 that they had agreed to the deal for Fabinho to move to England for a reported £39m fee. This deal was announced with little notification and there had been almost no rumours in the press surrounding the deal.

The lack of competition for the signature of Fabinho must have come as a surprise for the Liverpool hierarchy, especially given his importance to the side now in a team that has won the Champions League and the Premier League in consecutive seasons but again this is a sign that Liverpool were identifying and recruiting players at an extremely high level with their data focus.

Now we see the player who is so important to this Liverpool side under Jürgen Klopp with his physical capacity allowing him to dominate space without the ball and his ability to read the game and time his movements from deep positions to connect with the forward players in the final third providing an integral part of the attacking game plan.

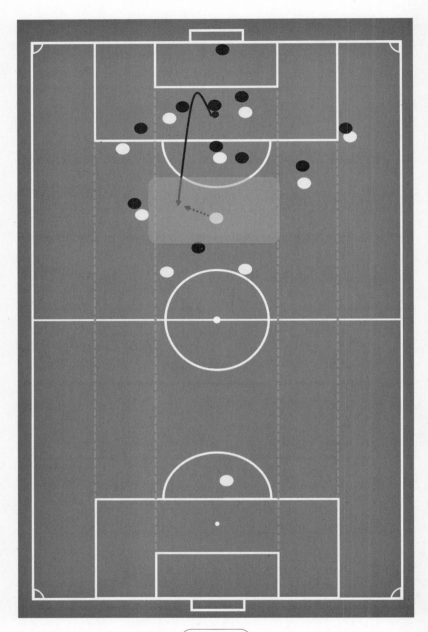

**Figure 51**

In *figure 51* we begin to see an example of why Fabinho is such an important player for Liverpool in terms of providing cover for teammates who move into higher positions on a regular basis. The Brazilian international provides an excellent base for the attack because of his mobility and the range that he has to recover possession should the opposition manage to clear the ball. This also extends to his ability to take up positions that, while still acting as a base to the attack, offer support to the man in possession to allow the ball to be switched backwards in order to change the point of the attack.

Here, we see an example where Liverpool have committed significant resources into the attack with five players positioned either in or on the edge of the penalty area and others moving into supporting positions.

The positioning of the bulk of the Liverpool attackers in high areas of the pitch has a natural consequence of forcing the opposition to collapse back into a poor defensive structure with little depth. This means that when the ball is cleared out of the penalty area there are not enough opposition players to effectively collect the clearance and move the ball forwards.

This is where we see Fabinho at his best as he moves into position to intercept the clearance before starting the second phase of the attacking movement and trying to find a route through into the opposition penalty area.

The ability of Fabinho to cover large parts of the final third and to win the ball back in transition allows Liverpool to play in a much higher attacking structure.

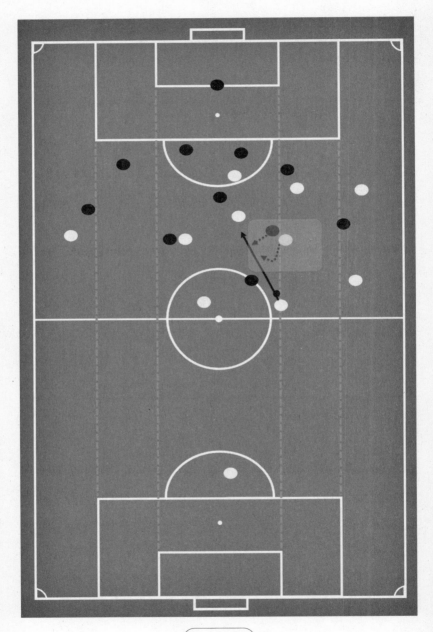

**Figure 52**

While controlling space is a key function that Fabinho provides for this Liverpool side, so is his ability to counter-press quickly and aggressively to win possession back for his side high up the pitch. We have already touched upon the importance of pressing and counter-pressing in an earlier chapter and these key defensive functions are important parts of the way that Fabinho plays the game.

In *figure 52* we see an example of the Brazilian international counter-pressing in order to win the ball back as quickly as possible. With Joël Matip in possession of the ball, his intent is to find the line-breaking pass through to a team-mate who has dropped back towards the ball in order to provide a passing option.

In this instance, however, the pass is relatively poor and a covering opposition player is able to shift across to intercept and win back the ball for his team. At the point of the interception, the defensive line for Liverpool is vulnerable. A key part of the attacking game model for Liverpool under Klopp sees them commit a lot of players into advanced areas quickly when they are in possession of the ball and while this can be effective for them in finding ways to quickly outplay the opposition defensive structure it can also lead to them being without cover.

This lack of defensive cover is, of course, mitigated somewhat by Liverpool having players with the physical profiles of Virgil van Dijk and Fabinho, players who have the range to cover space and the intelligence and intuition to read danger before it develops.

In this example, as the opposition player intercepts the ball we see Fabinho react to get back around from his attacking position to challenge and win the ball back before the first pass is even played. These moments of chaos are when having a player in this controlling position is so important for Liverpool.

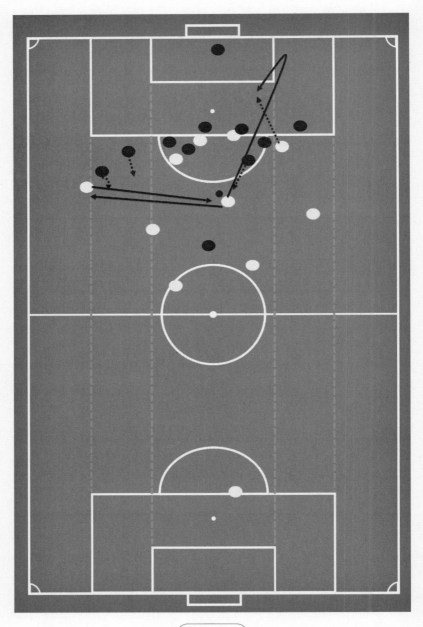

**Figure 53**

In *figure 53* we see another example of Fabinho being in position to recover the ball before then accessing the penalty area.

This time, when Fabinho collects possession the opposition are compact across the line of the penalty area and there is no space that can be opened. Instead of just looking to put the ball back into the penalty area he remains calm and composed and plays a quick combination of passes with the left-back who is positioned on the same line as him.

These passes have a dual intention as Liverpool maintain possession but they also pull the opposition out towards him. As the opposition move out to press the ball we see Fabinho able to receive the ball back before then playing the pass beyond the defensive line. This time the ball is played over the defensive line towards the far side of the penalty area where an attacking player has pulled off to make the run.

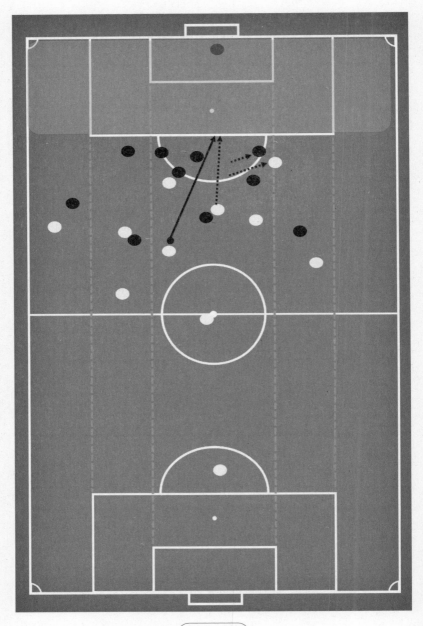

**Figure 54**

While Fabinho provides an important function for this Liverpool side with his work and positioning when out of possession that does not mean that he is not an integral part of the structure with his ability to play progressively when in possession.

We see this in *figure 54* as Fabinho has possession at the edge of the final third. One of the most important functions of any midfield player is to play passes that break the lines of the opposition. This allows the ball to be progressed forward efficiently and creates overloads that can break down the opposition defensive structure.

The space is initially created as Mohamed Salah moves out towards the far side of the penalty area; this small movement pulls the defender out of position and creates a gap in the defensive line. Now, Fabinho is able to play the vertical pass through the defensive block to access that space. That one pass takes all of the outfield players on the pitch out of the game and creates an opportunity in the penalty area as Firmino moves forward to collect the ball.

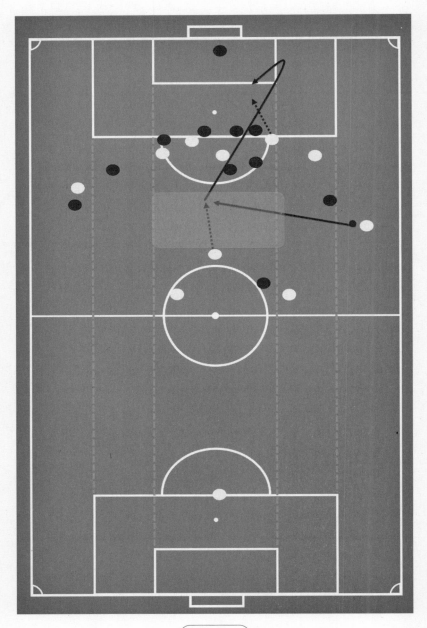

**Figure 55**

Fabinho also impressed with his understanding of when and how to join the attacking movement, as we can see in *figure 55*. Liverpool are positioned high across the width of the penalty area and once again this has forced the opposition defensive back to defend this space.

The ball is switched across to Alexander-Arnold on the right-hand side of the pitch and as the right-back receives the ball he is initially in space, although an opposition player quickly moves out to engage the ball. This movement to press the ball prevents it from being quickly played back into the penalty area.

At this point, we see Fabinho, who is positioned initially in a deeper position where he can cover space defensively. With no route into the penalty area, we see Fabinho move forward into the central space to receive the pass as it is moved inside by Alexander-Arnold. As the Brazilian accepts possession in this area he again looks to lift a pass into the space between the opposition defensive line and goalkeeper.

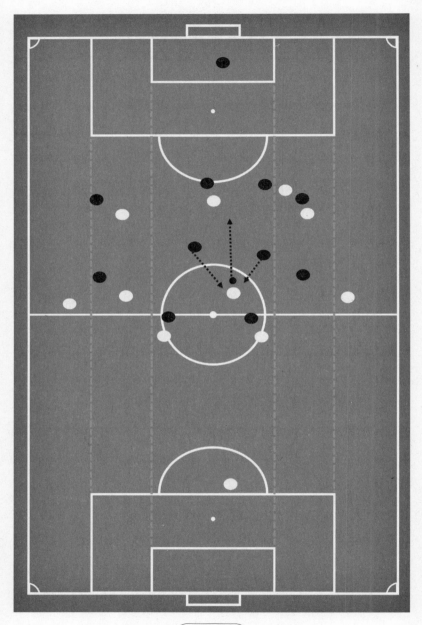

**Figure 56**

A large part of what makes Fabinho such an effective presence is his all-round skill set. He is fantastic out of possession when pressing or cutting passing lanes but he is also effective in possession when breaking the lines of just taking up positions that allow the ball to be circulated.

Given his physical profile, however, Fabinho is equally dangerous when receiving the ball and dribbling forward to engage and break the next line of opposition pressure. Fabinho has a long stride and he uses this effectively to move the ball beyond opposition players.

We see a clear example of this in *figure 56* as Fabinho has possession of the ball centrally. Two opposition players are pressing towards the ball and looking to engage Fabinho. The Brazilian international, however, is comfortable under pressure and he breaks past both players and moves beyond the four players in the midfield line. This immediately creates an opportunity for Liverpool to overload the defensive line.

## Chapter 11
# Naby Keïta

There is a sense amongst the Liverpool fanbase that they needed a midfield player who could carry the ball and break lines in order to take the team to the next level. That player was thought to be Naby Keïta and a deal was agreed in August 2017 for the Guinea international to join the club at the end of the 2017/18 season for a reported £48m from RB Leipzig. At this point, even with the high cost attached to the transfer, it was generally thought that Keïta represented the missing link for Klopp and that his signing would be the catalyst that would take Liverpool on to the next level.

Before we discuss the kind of player profile that led to people thinking in that way and before we discuss the barriers that have so far impeded Keïta in England it is useful to consider his career progression to this point.

It is interesting to note that a large part of the development of Keïta as a player happened when he was at Red Bull Salzburg (RBS) in Austria. This was despite moving initially from his native Guinea to France where he played in the second tier with a relatively small club called FC Istres. Now, any young player with potential like Keïta would likely be signed by the Austrian side directly from Western Africa without the need for another stop in Europe first. The success of players like Keïta along with Diadie Samassékou and Amadou Haidara has seen RBS concentrate their recruitment efforts in this region.

That Keïta played domestic football in Guinea and made the move to France without having a contract in place suggests that at this stage the region was not as extensively covered as it is now. While the young midfielder did land a contract with FC Istres he was turned down after going through trials at both Lorient and Le Mans; it is likely that both of those clubs greatly regret their decision. In his one season in French football, Istres were actually relegated from the second tier, although Keïta impressed hugely with his performances in the centre of the midfield as he looked to drive his side forward time and time again.

These performances made it unlikely that Keïta would still be with Istres when they began their third season in the top flight and this proved to be the case with RBS with the fee reported to be under £1.5m. It was during his time with RBS that Keïta began to make a real impact on the public consciousness as he dominated games from his position as the left-sided central midfielder in either a midfield diamond or as a three. Keïta was starting to develop into the perfect modern midfield player with a very specific skill set. His ability to carry the ball through the midfield with driving progressive runs was particularly important for the Austrian side given that they have a tendency to dominate matches and therefore they face a lot of deep and compact defensive blocks. Having a player like Keïta who could take possession centrally before driving past the closest defender created havoc in the opposition defensive structure. In these central areas beating an opposition defender immediately forces another opponent to break from their defensive position to engage with the ball. This, in turn, creates space that attacking players can exploit around the penalty area.

In the end, Keïta's time in Austria only lasted for two seasons before he made the predictable move to another of the Red Bull sides as he crossed the border into Germany to join RB Leipzig for a reported £27m fee.

Once again we saw Keïta comfortably adapt his game to the next level of competition and again his style of play appeared ideally suited to the Bundesliga. Keïta's all-action style of play and his ability to press relentlessly when out of possession for long periods at a time were a perfect match for the style of play that RB Leipzig were looking to implement. In possession, though, his time in Germany elevated his game to the next level as Keïta became a dominant force in possession of the ball and began to create as well as score more goals than he had previously in his career.

It is no secret that the game model of the Red Bull clubs, yes we can describe RB Leipzig as a Red Bull club despite the fact that they are unable to use the title in Germany, is almost perfectly suited to the way that Jürgen Klopp prefers his Liverpool side to play. The aggressive pressing style out of possession and the willingness to play vertical attacking football with the ball are concepts that create players that fit the way that Klopp wants to play. It was, therefore, no surprise that Liverpool became one of the most active suitors for the Guinean midfielder when it became clear that RB Leipzig were willing to entertain offers for their star midfielder. Unlike the transfer of Fabinho, which was completed without fanfare or speculation, the deal to sign Keïta was more drawn out with rounds of intense negotiation. Eventually, as with the deal to sign Virgil van Dijk, the deal was completed with the midfielder being allowed to spend the remainder of the 2017/18 season at Leipzig before making the move to England.

We have already referenced above that Keïta is a perfect modern midfielder. His low centre of gravity and excellent balance allow him to receive and manipulate the ball in tight areas and he is extremely press resistant with his ability to hold off challenges and turn defenders allowing him to create space. Keïta is an extremely progressive player with the ability to carry the ball through the centre or play passes that break the lines of the opposition. His pass completion rate does not match that of many other midfield players but this is because he rarely looks for the safe pass. Instead, he takes possession of the ball and then looks for the forward pass whenever possible.

So, if Keïta meets all of the criteria that Liverpool are likely to want in a central midfield player then why has the Guinean international not been a success to this point at Anfield? The main issue has been that he has suffered consistent injury issues with a series of setbacks that have prevented him from putting together a run of matches at the first-team level. A series of strains and pulls have led to periods on the sidelines but these are not likely to have an impact on his ability to play week after week going forward, as long as Liverpool can learn to manage his workload in training.

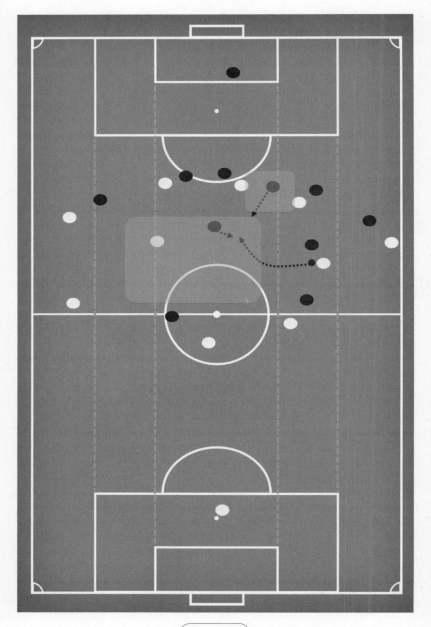

Figure 57

The introduction of Naby Keïta into the midfield block by Liverpool adds a completely new dimension to the way that Liverpool attack. While both Jordan Henderson and Georginio Wijnaldum are capable ball progressors and solid contributors when it comes to the recycling of possession neither possesses the threat that Keïta does to beat his direct opponent with a dribble.

This ability to engage and beat a defensive player in a 1v1 situation centrally completely alters the dynamic of the game and can be the catalyst for Liverpool breaking through compact defensive structures.

*Figure 57* gives us an example of this with Keïta in possession of the ball in the right half-space with one opposition midfielder looking to engage him and close down the available space. Keïta is one of the most press-resistant midfielders in the top level and he tends to wait in possession to allow the defensive players to initiate contact. When this initial contact is made we see Keïta manipulate the ball past the pressing player and he uses his low centre of gravity to pivot around and move into space. Once he is past a player in this kind of area he is able to use his burst of acceleration to move away and attack the available space.

Now, consider the impact that this kind of movement can have in this Liverpool side. With the likes of Sadio Mané, Mohamed Salah and Roberto Firmino already occupying central areas you now have a player like Keïta moving with momentum into the final third from where he can create attacking overloads.

In this particular example, as Keïta moves past his man he attracts two other defenders towards him. This creates the overload opportunity either centrally or on the edge of the penalty area.

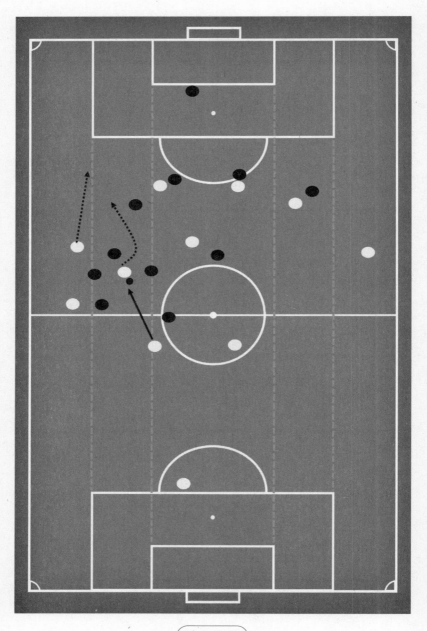

**Figure 58**

We have already discussed the fact that Keïta is extremely press resistant and this allows him to receive the ball when already under pressure from the opposition. The ability to accept possession of the ball despite the presence of defensive players behind can be key when playing against sides who display a tendency to defend deep. It can also help Liverpool when they are building through the thirds against a side that are comfortable trying to press them.

We see an example of this in *figure 58* as the ball is played into the feet of Keïta as he is effectively surrounded by three defensive players who are looking to prevent him from moving the ball forward. The pass back to the first line is open but Keïta is an extremely progressive player and he will look for the ball forward whenever possible.

Once again, we see Keïta pause in possession of the ball to initiate contact and as one of the defensive players gets too close the Guinea international rolls past him and then accelerates through the gap between the players who are looking to engage the press.

This small movement was enough to completely break the opposition press and take all of these players who were happy engaging higher out of the game.

As Keïta moves beyond the press he is in the half-space and the nearest defender is already occupied through the positioning of Mané. Couple this with the movement from Robertson to get forward to provide the width and the defender is suddenly in a 1v3 situation.

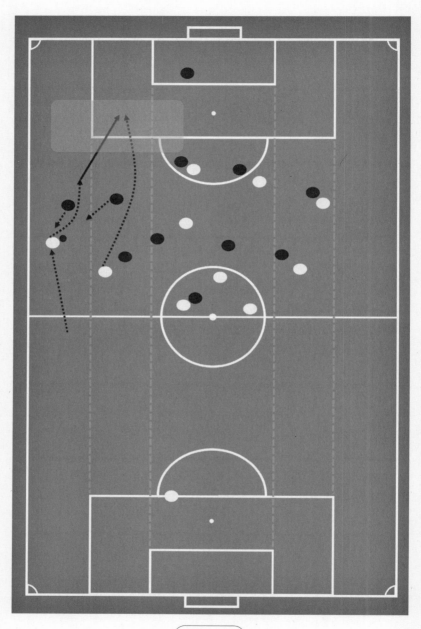

**Figure 59**

*Figure 59* gives us another example of how effective Naby Keïta is at carrying the ball and breaking through the defensive lines of the opposition. This time he has moved out to the wide area on the left-hand side of the pitch. He carries the ball forwards until he reaches a defensive player looking to block the run and engage with the press.

At this point, we simply see another favourite move from Keïta as he drops his shoulder and moves beyond the defender at pace. This movement immediately creates a dangerous situation that Keïta can look to take advantage of and he attracts another player towards the ball as they look to stop Keïta from progressing any further.

Now, if we stop for a second and consider the situation, we have the ball entering the final third and one defensive player is already beaten while another has been pulled out of his defensive slot. Combine this with the fact that Robertson looks to make a run underneath to underlap the defender who has been pulled out of the slot and it quickly becomes clear that Liverpool are positioned to break past the defensive line on this side of the pitch.

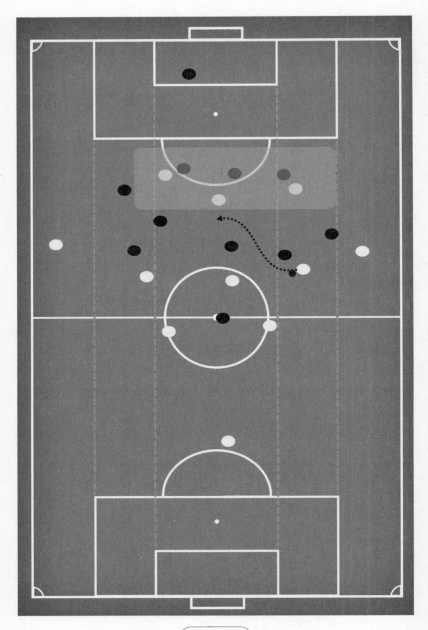

**Figure 60**

Naby Keïta is comfortable playing in different positional slots across the midfield line but his ability to beat people stays the same whether he is having to drive past defensive players on the right or the left side.

In *figure 60* we can see Keïta in possession of the ball, originally in the right half-space and once again there is a player in close proximity who is looking to engage quickly in the press. As Keïta takes possession he quickly moves past the defensive player and cuts inside. This time, however, he does not stop at beating one player and as the second defensive player moves to close him down Keïta moves easily past him. Once again we immediately see that this movement from Keïta, that has taken him beyond two defensive players, has created a central overload in the final third. Now Liverpool are in a position to break through the defensive line and into the penalty area.

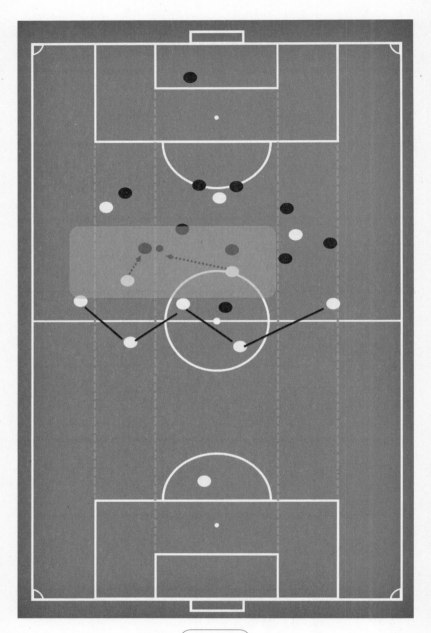

**Figure 61**

Out of possession Keïta also has a different profile to Wijnaldum and this difference changes the profile of the midfield when Keïta is positioned on the left of the midfield three. While Wijnaldum blocks passing lanes and holds the defensive shape, Keïta is more likely to press and engage the ball carrier in higher areas of the pitch.

When coupled with Jordan Henderson, who also presses higher and thrives in the transition, this changes the profile of the Liverpool midfield completely. We see this in the situation shown in *figure 61* as the opposition are building an attack with possession of the ball in the midfield area. We see Fabinho, acting as the '6', is still in a relatively deep position having formed a defensive line of five. This allows Keïta, on the left, and Henderson, on the right, to move out and engage the ball carrier. Having developed at the Red Bull clubs Keïta is a player who is used to pressing aggressively and he does so while also using his body to prevent the ball from being moved past him easily.

## Chapter 12
# Sadio Mané

It is interesting within these chapters to note that so many of Liverpool's key players have progressed their careers through a series of sensible steps that have allowed them to progress at each tier before reaching the top level with Liverpool. The likes of Virgil van Dijk and Naby Keïta have done this and so too has the subject of this chapter, Sadio Mané. The fact that so many players who have not only reached the top level but have played with such consistent success have taken this measured approach to their career development shows that this approach is one that could be emulated by young players who are still at the development stage.

Sadio Mané, in particular, has followed a path that is a familiar one for young players who start their development journey in Western Africa. As a youngster, he played in his local leagues where his talent stood out nearly immediately. Eventually, he moved to Generation Foot, one of the most prestigious football academies in the whole of Africa. Here, the young attacker got his first exposure to professional training techniques and his prodigious work rate in training coupled with his incredible potential saw him singled out early as a player who was likely to have a future in European football. In the end, Mané only spent a matter of months at the academy before making the move to join Metz in France. At the time Metz had a partnership agreement in place with Generation Foot that saw them given an early warning when a young player was coming through and showing promise. This move, from Western Africa to France is one the best steps for a developing player given the similarities in language and Metz provided a sensible next step to expose Mané to a more difficult level of competition. For all of these positives, however, Mané was still not a Metz player for long and he ended up spending just one season at the French side before making the next logical progression in his career. That progression saw Mané move to Austria to join Red Bull Salzburg (RBS) in a deal worth £3.6m. We have already discussed in a previous chapter the fact that RBS are now more active in their recruitment within Western Africa as a region. Mané, along with Naby Keïta, will have played a significant role in that change in focus from the Austrian side. The ability to identify players at source and cut out the initial move to European football represents the chance to save a significant amount of money for RBS.

In Austria, we began to see Mané develop into a more complete football player. He played under the German coach Roger Schmidt who is famous for his extreme high-pressing style. The Senegalese forward has been open in the past about the fact that Schmidt helped him to develop the tactical side of his game. Up until this point Mané had largely played to his strengths and used his pace to create moments of separation between himself and the opposition defenders. Now, at RBS we saw Mané exposed to tactical concepts like overloading and underloading and when out of possession he learnt how to execute pressing traps. All of these aspects of Mané's overall game are clearly evident in the player that we see today at Anfield and they were learnt in Austria. While at RBS the performances of Mané were not going unnoticed, although the perceived lack of quality in the Austrian league did lead to some believing that Mané may struggle to adapt his game to a higher level. Luckily for Mané, and as it turned out for Liverpool, there was one Premier League side who had seen enough from Mané to be convinced of his quality, Southampton.

Sadio Mané made the move to English football for a reported fee of £20.7m. It very quickly became apparent that fears over the attacker's ability to adapt to the pace of the English game were unfounded and he quickly established himself as one of the key players in the Southampton squad. Once again, however, we saw Mané spend only two seasons at this level before moving to an elite club. That move saw Mané follow what was increasingly becoming a familiar route as he moved to Liverpool for a fee in the region of £37m.

Once again the step up in quality proved to be no problem to Mané. His pace and direct running from the left-hand side of the pitch added a new dimension to the side and his ability to find and occupy spaces in the final third and to link the play between the forwards and midfielders became a key feature of how they looked to attack and break teams down.

The importance of Mané to Liverpool is further highlighted by his underlying metrics so far this season as he is averaging 0.57 goals per 90 minutes from an expected goals value of 0.46 per 90. This means that Mané is scoring on average over one goal every two games. Perhaps more telling, though, are the other metrics that give an insight into Mané's style of play and his effectiveness. He is averaging, at the time of writing, 4.96 dribbles per 90 and perhaps more importantly 5.57 touches in the opposition box per 90. This tells us that in possession Mané is progressive in his willingness to take the ball and run at the opposition defence but also that with his movements from outside to in he is getting into position to receive the ball in the opposition penalty area. To put it further into context, 5.57 touches in the opposition box per 90 is second only to 6.69 from Salah.

For all that Mohamed Salah is given the lion's share of the plaudits for his goalscoring exploits we have to recognise how effective and how efficient Sadio Mané is as a part of this Liverpool attack.

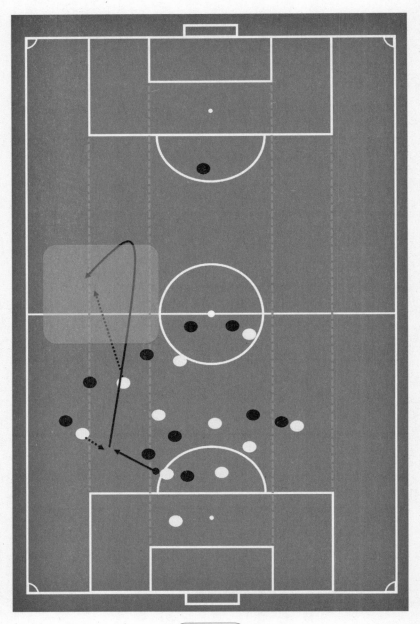

**Figure 62**

We have previously touched upon the fact that of the two wide forward players Mané is far more active in the defensive phase and this translates to the way that he helps this Liverpool team in moments of transition.

His pace and ability to carry the ball past opposition players are a great release mechanism that allows Liverpool to transition quickly from the defensive phase to the attacking phase. When Liverpool are defending they tend to leave Salah and Firmino in more advanced areas while the left-hand side of the pitch tends to be open. We see an example of these transitions in *figure 62* as Liverpool win the ball back deep inside their own half of the field.

As Virgil van Dijk takes possession of the ball he has no obvious vertical passing options because of the positioning of the opposition attacking players. Instead, left-back, Robertson, moves in towards the ball and connects with Van Dijk to take possession, so now the vertical passing lane is open.

Robertson plays the ball into space along this lane and immediately we see that Mané is accelerating into this open space. As Mané takes possession he is challenged by a defensive player but his momentum allows him to knock the ball down the outside of the defender and immediately Liverpool have transitioned from a defensive situation to having a chance on goal. These are very deliberate tactical choices that we see from Liverpool as they are not in any way possession orientated. Instead, they look constantly for opportunities to play that vertical pass that stretches the opposition defensive block and in Mané they have a forward player who is an ideal fit for that vertical passing style of play.

While Mané does take up central positions he has a tendency to do so on slightly deeper lines than Mohamed Salah out on the right side. This is a deliberate action in most cases which is intended to allow Mané to already have momentum with his forward movement as he reaches the defensive line. This plays perfectly to his strength of bursting through gaps in the opposition defensive structure.

We see an example of this kind of action in *figure 63* with Mané positioned in the left half-space on a notably deeper line than Salah and Firmino. As the ball begins to be progressed from the back, Mané is in a position to accept possession via a simple diagonal pass that accesses the space. As ever, the first thought that Mané has when taking possession of the ball in these areas is to turn and drive at the defensive line. As he moves higher up the field a defender tries to engage but because Mané started deeper he is already reaching top speed and can simply move past the challenge. Even now, as he drives into the penalty area, and as the goalkeeper comes out to challenge for the ball, Mané displays his selfless side by flicking the ball centrally to an area that is occupied by the other forward players instead of trying to finish himself from a difficult angle.

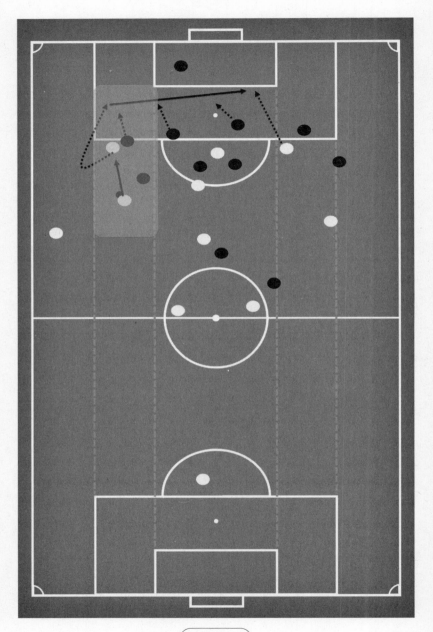

**Figure 64**

In *figure 64* we again see how effective Mané is when positioned in these half-spaces but this time his starting point is much higher up the field. Liverpool are in a sustained attacking action and the opposition in this match, Spurs, have dropped very deep to try to defend their penalty area.

As the man in possession, Wijnaldum, looks forward he can see no easy way to access the penalty area and he looks to connect with a short vertical pass to Mané, positioned just ahead of the ball, to see if this tempts some of the Spurs players to break out of their defensive shape.

As Mané receives the ball, however, he does not wait for the defender to move out and instead fakes to move back with the ball before exploding down the outside of the nearest defender, Davinson Sanchez. As he does so he has turned a slow and difficult attacking movement into an opportunity with the ball behind the defensive line. As he moves into this space the other forward players are making runs towards the edge of the six-yard box and the ball is cut back inside to create a goalscoring opportunity.

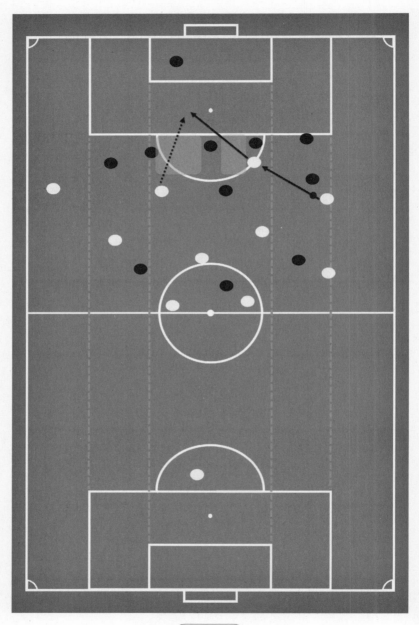

Figure 65

In *figure 65* we see yet another example of Mané starting his attacking run from a deeper position and using this to break free beyond the defensive line of the opposition.

The attacking movement for Liverpool starts on the right-hand side and Firmino and Salah have switched positions. As the Brazilian receives the ball his first thought is to move progressively and play forwards; remember one of the key tactical concepts that we see from Liverpool is verticality, and he immediately feeds the ball into the feet of Salah who is central.

There are still some who believe that Salah is a greedy or selfish player who does not pass often enough. The truth is that he often takes possession of the ball in areas where, with his quality, he is able to create the opportunity for a shot at goal. Here we see Salah slow the pace of the game down as he waits for support. Because of Mané's deeper starting position, he is already reaching speed as he passes Salah and when the pass is played through the defensive line we see Mané moving on to it unchallenged for a chance on goal.

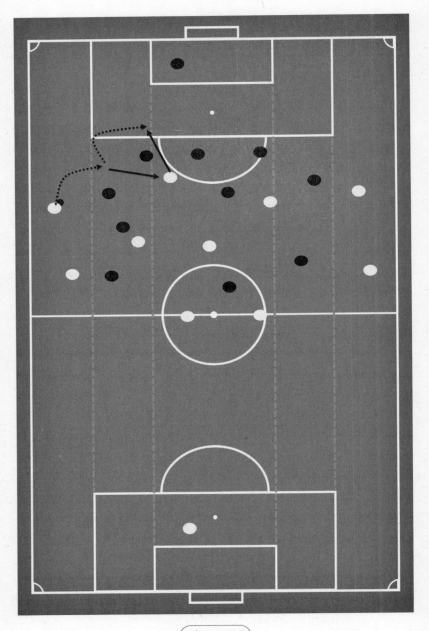

**Figure 66**

This time, in *figure 66*, we see Mané collect the ball in the wide area in space. Again, his first thought is to attack the defensive line. To do so he immediately engages and attacks the nearest defensive player and looks to drive past him on the outside. The key thing to note about Mané, though, is that even when travelling at something approaching top speed he is still capable of playing accurate combinations with team-mates. It is this combination of pace and intelligence in the final third that makes it so hard to defend against him.

We see this here as Mané drives past the defender and then approaches the penalty area. With one more defender in place to challenge he plays a lateral pass into the feet of Firmino while still moving at pace and collects the ball on the other side of the defender following a flick from the Brazilian.

Once again the pace of Mané moving from deeper areas has allowed him to access the penalty area.

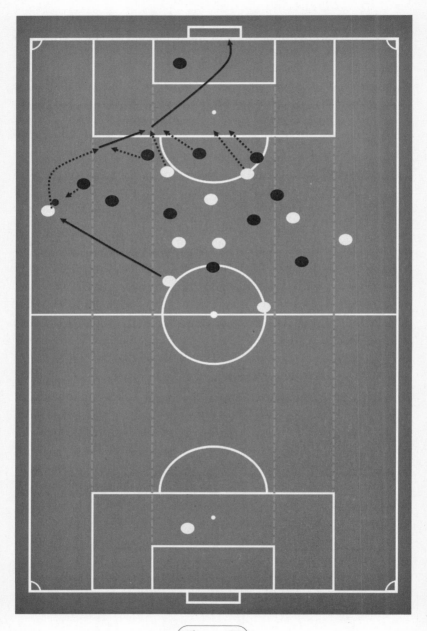

**Figure 67**

Our final example for this chapter shows again the importance of the half-space as Liverpool move forward in possession. We see this in *figure 67*. On this occasion, Mané is not actually involved in the attacking move until the end when he finishes a chance on goal.

The play starts with a Liverpool free-kick and Virgil van Dijk passes out to the left side where Robertson is positioned to give width.

Robertson is positive in possession and he moves down the outside towards the edge of the opposition penalty area. Having moved past one defensive player, a second player moves out to engage the ball. Again, we see the effectiveness of Liverpool having players who can beat a player in the final third; this form of attacking movement consistently forces other attacking players out of position.

As the second defender moves out to engage with the ball we see Mané drift into the space that the defender has vacated. A simple pass inside accesses this space and as Mané receives the ball he opens his body out and curls the ball into the opposite side of the goal.

# Chapter 13
# Mohamed Salah

Hindsight is a wonderful thing, especially in the context of football. How often have we seen players essentially discarded by clubs as they do not feel that the player in question meets the standards of the club or league, only for the player to develop at their new club and suddenly meet their potential? In recent seasons Chelsea have been one of the worst examples of this having released the likes of Kevin De Bruyne and Romelu Lukaku for what would turn out to be a fraction of their future value. To that list, we can add the Egyptian international forward Mohamed Salah who Chelsea originally brought to the Premier League from the Swiss side Basel before failing to provide him with adequate first-team opportunities.

Out of all of the players who are currently in this Liverpool side it is potentially Salah who best represents the work of the data-driven recruitment department. As the 2016/17 season was drawing to a close Liverpool were working on potential targets who could strengthen the front line. Jürgen Klopp had his own player in mind and he wanted the club to pursue the Bayer Leverkusen attacker Julian Brandt, a young German attacker who typically played from the left-hand side of a front three. This was, of course, also the best position and role of Sadio Mané.

The recruitment department, however, was unanimous in their belief that the correct signing would in fact be Mohamed Salah with the Egyptian forward having impressed over the course of the season in Serie A with Roma.

While some other players in Liverpool's squad have taken measured steps in their career and have moved through the stages incrementally with time spent adapting at each level before they move on we have seen Salah take a more circuitous route to the top.

Mohamed Salah started his professional career in his native Egypt with El Mokawloon, making his debut in the first team at the age of 18, in 2010. Given what we know of Salah now it should come as no surprise that his talent did not go unnoticed but unlike the likes of Mané in Senegal there was no established pathway for North Africans to go to Europe. This simply meant that the Swiss side were able to position themselves to be the ones that brought Salah to Europe in 2012.

The Egyptian forward settled in Europe almost immediately and began impressing with his pace and ability to carry the ball beyond the opposition's defensive lines, although at this stage his finishing was at best raw. Even if the goals did not flow freely Salah still became a firm fan favourite in Switzerland and gradually his performances began to see scouts flocking to Basel matches to watch the forward in action. Even with the increased levels of interest, however, it still came as something of a surprise when after two seasons in Switzerland he moved to Chelsea for a fee that was thought to be in the region of £11m.

While the likes of Sadio Mané and Fabinho took incremental steps to reach the Premier League the same could not be said of Salah and after two years and no significant statistical output, the Egyptian forward found himself in the Premier League. Perhaps then it should not come as a surprise that Salah struggled to make a real impact at the first-team level for

Chelsea. His signing was part of an overt recruitment strategy that aimed to sign talented young players from across Europe and then use the loan system to find first-team football for them. This was the same strategy that saw the likes of Lukaku and De Bruyne signed and then parked elsewhere before they then left the club. It is also worth noting that at this point in time the coach at Chelsea was Jose Mourinho who notoriously preferred a small squad of first-team football and preferred experience over youth throughout the club. Despite this Salah did impress enough to play on 13 occasions for Chelsea over the course of his two years at the club. At that point, Salah became unsettled and believed that his development was stalling as a result of the lack of first-team football. He began to agitate for a move away from the club and eventually left to join Fiorentina in the January transfer window of 2015 in an 18-month loan move. It was in Florence that Salah truly began to develop into the player that we see today. His finishing and final ball began to develop fully to go along with his explosive movements around the penalty area. Everything seemed to finally be going well for the forward at this point and at the end of his first season in Italy the expectation was that he would play for the entirety of the next season in Florence. That was until Salah refused to return to Florence in time for the next season. The deal between Chelsea and Fiorentina was very much in place and both sides expected Salah to honour the loan.

This was the first point in his career that we truly saw the stubborn side of Salah and eventually the agreement with Fiorentina was cancelled, although Salah still came to play that season in Serie A as he made the move to Roma instead.

In Rome, Salah continued his excellent development as he built upon his performances over the previous six months with Fiorentina. At the end of that season, Roma made the transfer permanent in a deal that was worth £13.5m. In the end,

Chelsea made only a small profit on the transfer of a player who had spent years in their development system and was only 12 months away from being recognised as one of the best players in world football.

The 2016/17 season was a genuine breakthrough for Salah as he performed to such a level that his data shone like a beacon to the recruitment department of Liverpool. Not only was Salah now one of the most efficient attacking players in Europe, he was also capable of creating chances and, more importantly, space for others. Through only his positioning on the pitch, Salah attracted more and more defensive attention towards him and this naturally created space elsewhere on the pitch that could be accessed by his team-mates.

We started this chapter talking about retrospect and in that sense the decision from the Liverpool recruitment team, and Klopp, to sign Salah appears to have been entirely logical but Chelsea still look to have allowed two of the best players in the world, Salah and De Bruyne, to leave the club without allowing them the time or opportunity to become regular first-team players at the club. For all that we talk about the quality of recruitment at Liverpool at times, they benefit from the mistakes of others.

Now, at Liverpool Mohamed Salah has developed fully into one of the most dangerous and deadly finishers in world football. His statistical output is the profile of a world-class footballer. He is averaging 0.61 goals per 90 with 3.57 shots per 90 and 4.29 dribbles per 90, along with a team-leading 6.69 touches per 90 minutes in the opposition box. With Roberto Firmino dropping into deeper areas of the field it is down to Mané and Salah to occupy spaces in the opposition box and from these positions both players are deadly.

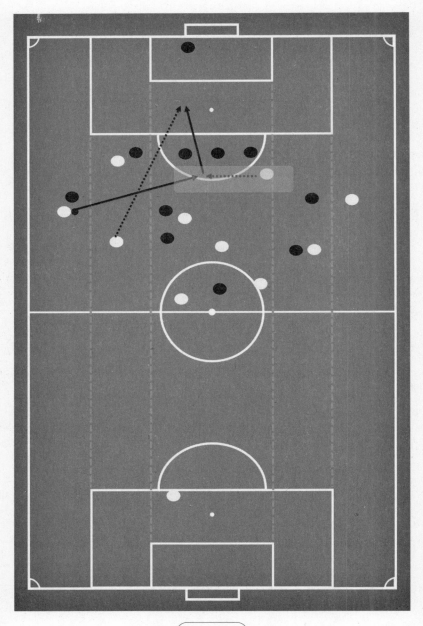

**Figure 68**

Such has been the impact that Mohamed Salah has had at Liverpool since his arrival that his positioning on the pitch is enough to affect the opposition. Such is the danger that the Egyptian carries that there tend to be multiple players checking his positioning as Liverpool build their attacking phase.

This allows Salah to create space for others and then to access that space through clever passing in the final third. There is still a sense that Salah is selfish in these areas but he is actually a very good link player with his ability to disguise passes and weight them perfectly.

We see an example of this in *figure 68* with Liverpool looking to break down a stubborn Bournemouth defensive block. The first pass is played across from Mané, on the left, with Salah having pulled out of centre slightly. This allows the Egyptian forward to move towards the ball in order to collect possession while moving into a central position. With no immediate pressure on the ball in this space, you would expect Salah to turn and shoot. Instead, Andy Robertson made a vertical run through the half-space and into the penalty area. As the left-back makes this run Salah times the pass through the defensive line perfectly to meet the run.

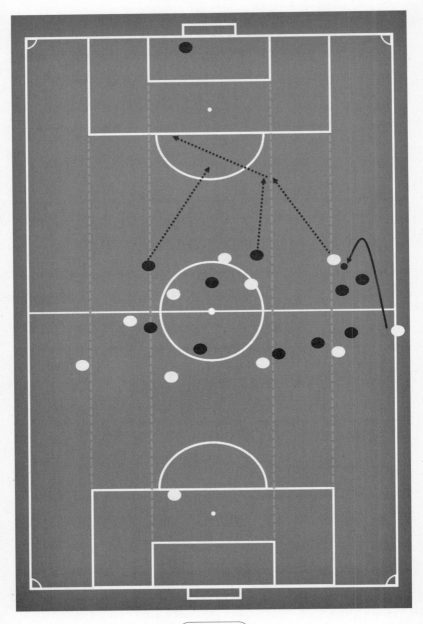

**Figure 69**

Salah makes no effort to defend other than pressing and counter-pressing the immediate transitions. Instead, he stays in central areas high up the field and essentially recovers his energy for when Liverpool win the ball back. When this does happen and when Liverpool move into their attacking phase we see Salah generally positioned to explode into space.

*Figure 69* shows an example of this as Liverpool have won a throw-in in the wide area. The throw is taken quickly and two opposition defenders get caught trying to win the ball; they both end up missing the header and the ball drops to Salah who is in space wide looking for an opportunity to pick up possession.

As soon as Salah does take possession of the ball and when he has space to move into he is single-minded in his intention to attack the penalty area as quickly as possible. We see this as he angles his run towards the penalty area. Two opposition players try to get into position to challenge for the ball but both times they are beaten by a simple misdirection when Salah shapes to shoot and then carries on his run on the same path.

While, as we have already seen, Salah is capable of interplay in the final third he is also one of the most single-minded and dangerous attacking players in world football when stretching the field through these vertical runs. Salah plays consistently on the highest line for Liverpool in areas that when he receives the ball he can turn and engage the defenders immediately. This is one of the key features of the concept of verticality that Klopp prefers when Liverpool are in possession.

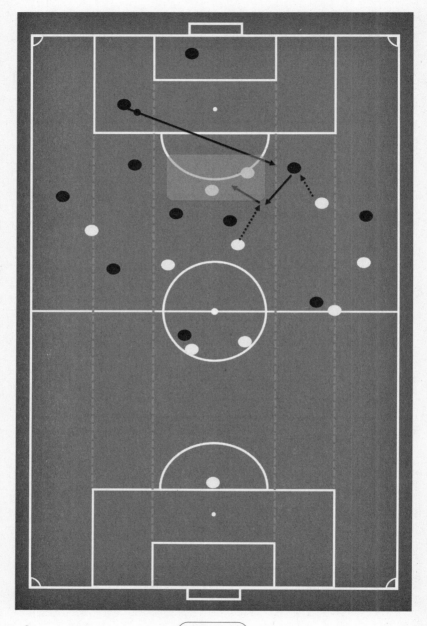

**Figure 70**

In *figure 70* we see again that Salah is happy to stay on a high line in the central areas when Liverpool are out of possession. This time, in the match against Wolves, the build-up from the opposition includes some strange, to say the least, choices. With the ball initially positioned in the penalty area, the Wolves player looks to play the ball across the face of goal and we can see that two Liverpool players, Salah and Firmino, are positioned centrally with no opposition player between them and the ball.

As the diagonal pass finds the Wolves player but given the nature of the pass, hard and slightly elevated, and the position of the receiving player, close to his own area and facing his own goal, the press is triggered and a Liverpool player engages to try to win the ball. The Wolves player manages to knock the ball on but before it can reach a Wolves player we see Jordan Henderson moving to engage and press high, as we have already seen throughout this book he is known to do. Henderson wins the ball and is able to shift it quickly to Salah in the central position.

Once again, while the Egyptian looks to be doing little work defensively he is simply taking up what was a perfect position to take advantage of the next attacking transition.

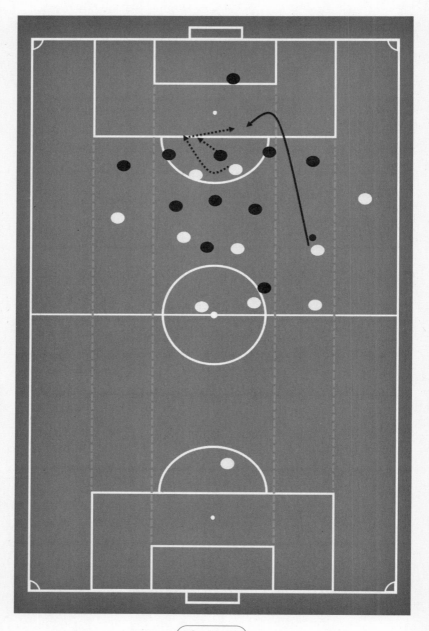

**Figure 71**

In *figure 71* we again see Salah positioned centrally, and not on the right side, against an opponent playing with a five man defence. This example shows the intelligence and technical ability of Salah to find space in tight areas.

As the ball breaks to Henderson, who is positioned in the right half-space, we see a lack of movement from Liverpool in the final third but with Henderson in possession Salah recognises that he might be able to create space for himself between the players in the defensive line.

The first movement from Salah is away from the ball. This takes him effectively on to the blindside of the defensive player that he is isolated against. This forces the defender to try to adjust so that he can cover and track the run that Salah is making. Henderson, having read the movement from Salah, plays a pass that drops into space between the defensive line and the goalkeeper. With the defensive player now unbalanced Salah completes his double movement to cut back across the defender and get on to the pass that is played through the line.

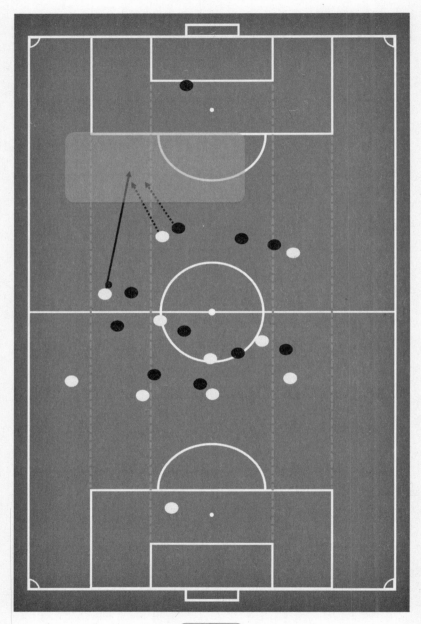

**Figure 72**

With Salah retaining a high position when Liverpool are out of possession the defensive block is obviously slightly unbalanced. While on the left-hand side we see Mané move back to provide cover for the left-back the same is not true on the right. To prevent Alexander-Arnold from being isolated defensively the range of Henderson and Fabinho in the midfield is key as both are capable of drifting across to the right side to help Alexander-Arnold as the ball goes over to this side.

For a coach like Klopp to allow this defensive imbalance, he has to be sure that the positives outweigh the negatives and this is certainly the case with Salah being able to position himself in advantageous areas where he can isolate a defensive player.

In *figure 72* we see a clear example of this as Liverpool look to move forward via a quick transition. The ball is shifted across to the left-hand side where Sadio Mané has found a vertical lane in which he can advance. As soon as the ball moves across the halfway line Salah starts to make a vertical movement looking to stretch the defensive line and to access space behind. Given that this situation has developed from an opposition set piece they are currently trying to recover their defensive position but Liverpool are attacking so quickly that the defensive player is still isolated. This is, again, an example of the verticality that Liverpool like to play with. As Mané takes possession he plays the angled ball forward into the path of Salah and the Egyptian forward is able to break away from the defender and make a move into the penalty area for a chance on goal.

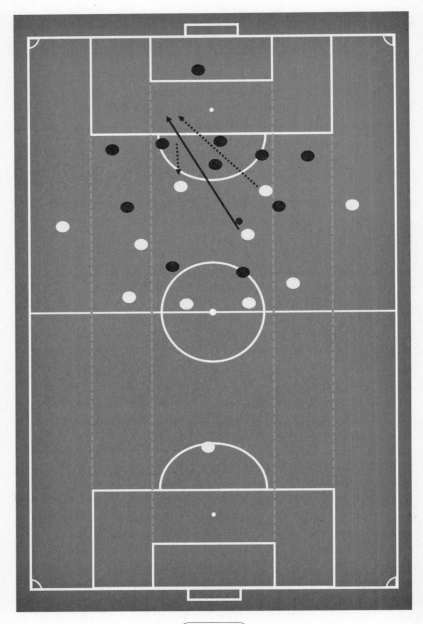

**Figure 73**

*Figure 73* is our final example in this chapter and it shows the effectiveness of the high/low movements that the Liverpool forwards use in order to break through a deep and passive defensive block. With the ball positioned centrally, where Sadio Mané has drifted into space, we see Salah positioned to the right of the ball while Firmino is in a central slot.

The defensive line of the opposition is trying to remain compact and they are showing no sign of wanting to move out to engage or press the ball. They are content to try to deny Liverpool the space in which they can play forward.

This is where the high and low movement comes into play. We know that Firmino prefers to drop back into the '10' space and he does so here as he moves towards the ball to give a passing option; again we can see that the backline is passive because there is no movement to follow Firmino out. This movement, however, does serve to at least distract the defenders and as Firmino is moving low we see Salah making a diagonal run to the high line beyond him. That run breaks through the defensive line and Mané has the quality on the ball to recognise this movement and execute the pass that allows Salah to get beyond the defensive line.

## Chapter 14

# Roberto Firmino

It is a mark of the tactical flexibility and ingenuity of this Liverpool side that the roles of the front three are almost completely inverted and this causes opposition defences no end of trouble. When your first-choice striker is responsible for linking play and creating and your wide forwards are responsible for occupying central areas and getting into positions to shoot at goal then you pose an interesting set of questions for the other teams' defensive game plans.

Of course, in order to have your striker drop into deeper positions and dictate the pace and angle of the attack effectively, you first have to find the *right* striker to do so. Luckily for Liverpool, their recruitment department was in a position to sign a player that fits this profile almost perfectly despite notable opposition from the head coach at the time, Brendan Rodgers. That player is the 28-year-old Brazilian international Roberto Firmino.

Roberto Firmino is the closest thing to a player at the elite level of football that we can say possesses a unique profile. He can create from central areas while either dropping deep or staying on the edge of the penalty area to receive the ball and link play from an advanced platform. He can press aggressively in the moments of transition or drop deep to cut off passing lanes and prevent the opposition from launching effective attacks. In other words, Firmino is capable of doing just about anything that you can ask him to do from a tactical perspective. While he is capable of performing all of these selfless and team-orientated tasks, however, that does not mean that he will operate in this way. Luckily for Liverpool Firmino is a player who always looks to put the team above his own interest. While the Brazilian international forward does not look to grab the headlines he is the key player behind those that do.

As with so many other players in this Liverpool squad, however, the path that Firmino took to reach the top was anything but conventional.

Initially, Firmino made his professional debut in his native Brazil but not with one of the traditional giants of the Brazilian game. Instead, Firmino made his breakthrough with Figueirense, but not in anywhere near the role that we see Firmino excel in now. Instead of playing as a forward player Firmino was utilised in a deeper defensive position. To an extent, we can see why this position and role would make sense for a player like Firmino. His composure on the ball and ability to bring others into play would be a key role in the build-up phase and his willingness to work constantly when out of possession would help in the defensive transition.

When Firmino did make the move to European football in 2011 it was to join a side that were just beginning to establish themselves in the German Bundesliga in Hoffenheim. Still, though, Firmino would not be used as a pure attacker. He was used in more advanced areas but more as a traditional '10' or as a wide attacker and always with a '9' who would act as the focus of the attacking movement of the side. In this sense, Firmino was now seen as more of a supporting player than one who would be the focal point in the team. That did not stop the supporters of the German side immediately taking to him with his blend of creativity and hard work, combining the values of the Brazilian and German games. Indeed, in many ways, Firmino possesses the mentality that we would traditionally associate with a German player. He has tricks aplenty and it is not unusual to see him attempt flicks and feints around the edge of the penalty area as he tries to create the space to shoot at goal; these tricks, however, are combined with a single-minded desire to work hard and to improve as a player.

Gradually, we saw Firmino establish himself as not only the key player at Hoffenheim but as one of the most exciting attacking players in Germany and this led to the Liverpool recruitment team looking to bring the Brazilian to England. Indeed, it was at this point that we first started to see the growing influence of the now sporting director Michael Edwards at the club. Edwards and his team wanted the team to sign Firmino to act as the focal point of the attack, whilst the coach at the time, Brendan Rodgers, wanted the club to pursue Aston Villa forward Christian Benteke. In the end, a compromise was reached and the club signed both but with the benefit of hindsight it is clear which decision proved better. Benteke struggled to find the back of the net and has continued to do so since moving on to Crystal Palace. Firmino, on the other hand, has become one of Liverpool's most important players.

At Liverpool, we have seen Firmino continue his tactical evolution as he has progressed from the base of the midfield to leading the line of the attack. While his creativity is still his key attribute, his ability in front of goal should not be discounted. There are few players in world football who possess his ability to recognise where space is being created in the opposition defensive structure. This ability to find space is coupled with the willingness to drift from his central position to take up a position in these spaces, and from these areas the Brazilian is able to affect play by either taking possession of the ball to his feet or simply standing still and pulling defensive players towards him. As soon as these players move towards the Brazilian they leave space behind them that can be exploited by the other attacking players in this Liverpool system.

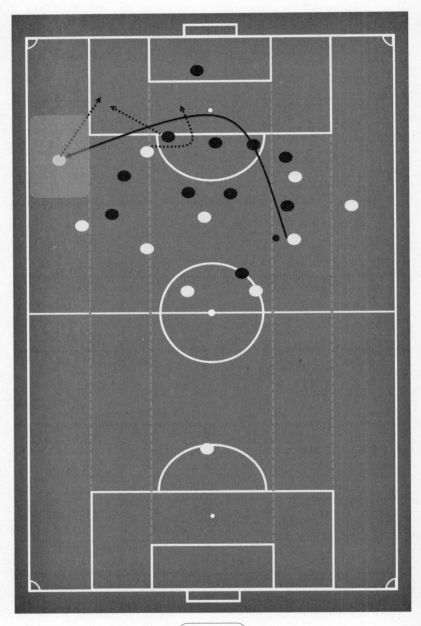

**Figure 74**

In *figure 74* we see an example of the kind of positional flexibility that we see from Firmino with his ability to drift into different areas of the pitch whether across the front third or back into the '10' space. This time the Brazilian striker has pulled out into the wide area allowing Mané to move centrally with Salah positioned to the right side.

As Firmino collects the ball he is completely free and he attacks the penalty area at an angle. This movement drags the nearest opposition defender towards him and this, in turn, leaves Mané in space near the front post. As Firmino moves towards the touchline the defender engages him but the Brazilian moves one way and then the other and is able to play the ball to the near post where Mané is now positioned.

So much of the attacking efficiency of Liverpool is down to the positions that Firmino takes up on the pitch. His ability to find space to receive the ball invariably attracts opposition defenders out to the ball and then creates opportunities for team-mates to exploit space themselves.

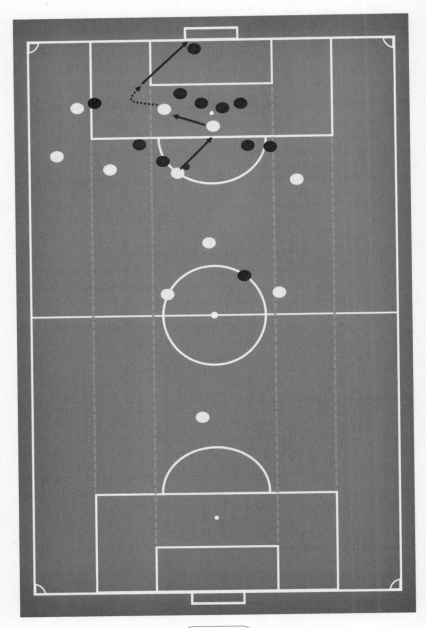

**Figure 75**

Out of all of the players in the Liverpool team, there are perhaps no others, with the exception of Salah, who are as creative and capable in tight spaces. We see an example of this in *figure 75* from a match against Tottenham Hotspur. There is no space in the penalty area as Liverpool work their way into the 18-yard-box but Liverpool still manage to access the space to create a shot at goal.

The ball initially moves centrally to Salah who then circulates the ball to Firmino on the left side. As the Brazilian receives the ball he allowsit to run past the defender before shifting quickly beyond the defensive line. In these areas the ability to manipulate the ball in tight spaces is key and Firmino connects and creates chances on a regular basis.

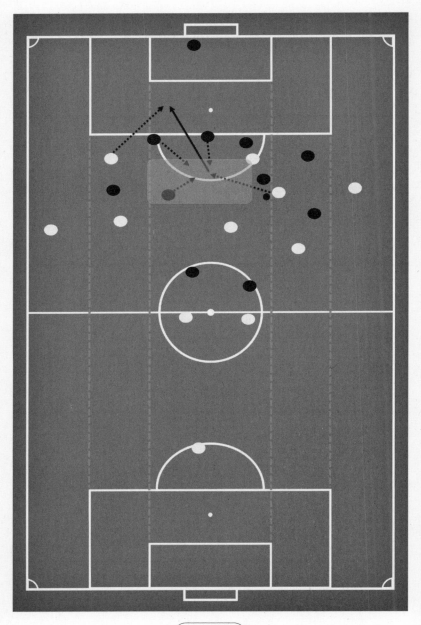

**Figure 76**

When Firmino drops into deep areas he is dangerous both in terms of his ability to create in possession and in terms of his ability to create space for others. We see an example of his dangerous ability in possession in *figure 76*.

Having dropped back into the central spaces we see that Salah has moved higher into a central position with Mané being wide on the left-hand side. Firmino could look to connect with other players moving from deeper positions. Instead, Firmino isolates and outplays the closest defensive player before moving into space behind them, and in front of the defensive line. Now, having accessed that space Firmino immediately starts to attract defensive attention with three players moving towards the Brazilian to engage the ball and press.

These movements immediately create opportunities for Liverpool to overload the defensive line. Firmino does so by slipping a through ball to the left side into the penalty area where Mané is moving diagonally on to the ball.

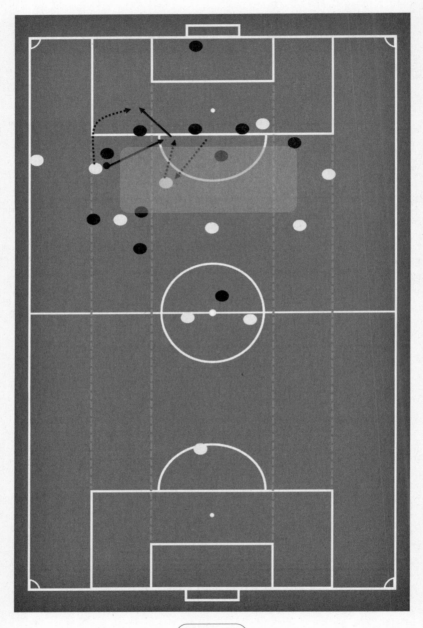

**Figure 77**

There are no strikers in football at the moment who connect as effectively as Firmino does for Liverpool and we see a clear example of this in *figure 77*. The movement from high to low from Firmino again proves to be key.

Salah has pulled over to the far post where he is looking to isolate a defensive player on the blind side, away from the ball, and Mané is positioned to the corner of the penalty area in possession of the ball. Firmino makes an initial movement off of the front line into the deeper area. When he takes up that position he is free from defensive attention and he moves back towards the penalty area into a position in which he can connect with Mané.

This initial movement off of the front line is the part of the movement that creates separation and allows Firmino to then help the progression of the ball.

As he moves back towards the penalty area Mané plays a lateral pass to the Brazilian who then plays the ball past the defensive line. This pass allows Mané to move diagonally past the defensive line and the opportunity is created on goal. These movements and interchanges are essential in helping Liverpool to break down compact defensive blocks.

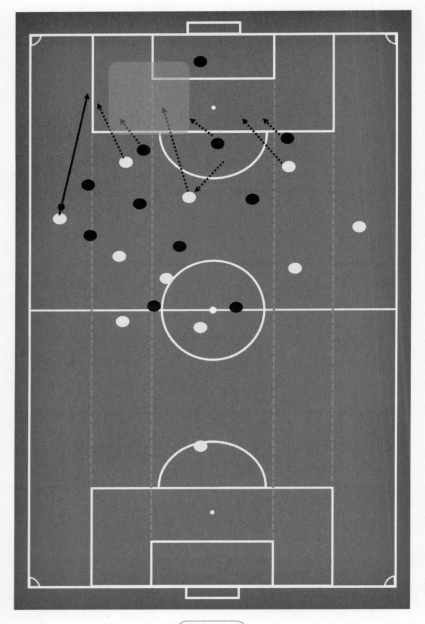

**Figure 78**

In *figure 78* we again see a moment in which Firmino made the low to high movement against a stubborn defensive side, this time in the Champions League tie against Red Bull Salzburg. As Liverpool are playing down the left-hand side of the pitch, Robertson is in possession and he plays a simple pass down the outside into space for Mané to move to a higher line.

As Mané moves on to the ball he drags a defensive player out with him to defend in the wide space. Liverpool had been trying to find a way to break through the defensive block but the Austrian side were exceptionally well drilled in the defensive phase.

Now, as the ball is worked into the wide areas the movement from Firmino, into the deeper space, has given the Brazilian freedom. As Mané moves down the wide area it is Firmino who makes an accurate vertical run that splits the defensive block and when the ball is played in towards the front post it is Firmino who is in position to shoot at goal. While previously we have seen that Mané makes these delayed runs from deeper areas at speed, Firmino, on the other hand, looks to move into the area from deeper areas almost unnoticed, not relying on pace but on the timing of his run.

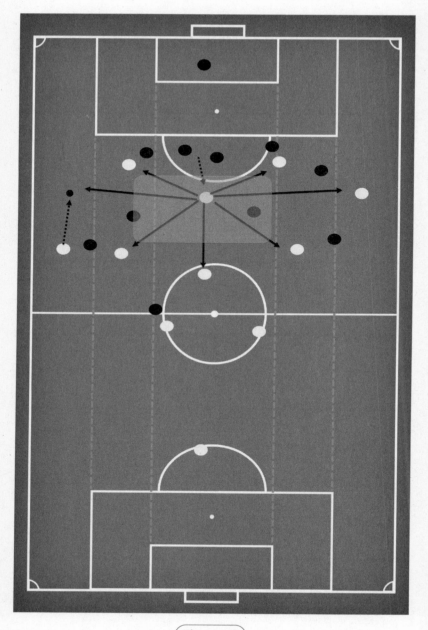

**Figure 79**

As a reference point for the attack, Roberto Firmino plays a role that is absolutely integral for the success of this Liverpool side. In *figure 79* we see why this is the case.

Having dropped into the '10' space we see the rest of the Liverpool players in their typical attacking structure. As you can see, Firmino is positioned centrally with the ability to access all areas of the field across the final third and deeper. On this occasion, the ball was switched wide to the left side of the pitch where Robertson was able to move high to collect possession. By dropping back into spaces off of the front line in this manner Firmino is able to take possession of the ball and to link with the rest of the attacking structure.

# 15.

# Anatomy of a goal

As we reach the end of this book I hope that you have gained an understanding of some of the tactical concepts that make Liverpool such a difficult team to play against.

For this chapter, I have highlighted and annotated seven goals that have been scored by Liverpool over the course of the 2019/20 season. Each of these goals shows the concepts that we have discussed throughout the book and highlights the kind of positions that Liverpool players take up on the pitch.

It is worth noting that these goals are not, in any way, ranked and they do not represent the 'best' goals that Liverpool have scored in any way, shape or form. Instead, they are interesting from a tactical point of view for various reasons.

As with anything else in football, the understanding of tactical concepts can add depth and colour to your enjoyment of a match but the match itself can also stand alone.

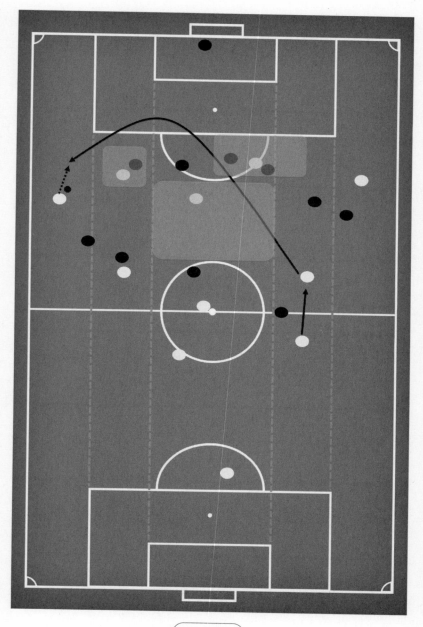

Figure 80

**Figure 81**

## Goal One: Mohamed Salah vs West Ham

Our first goal was scored, perhaps fittingly, by Mohamed Salah as the Egyptian displayed his awareness in the penalty area to create room and finish a cut back from Andy Robertson. *Figure 80* shows the occupation of space from the front three of Liverpool with Mané, on the left of the attack, and Salah, on the right, isolated against defensive players who are effectively pinned in place while centrally Firmino has dropped off into a deeper position.

As the ball is played forward to Alex Oxlade-Chamberlain, just inside the opposition half, the switch of play is open to Robertson as Mané has dragged the opposition full-back inside with him.

When this pass is executed the complexion of the move changes.

*Figure 81* shows the continuation of this move as Robertson takes his touch forward and is able to break into the penalty area at an angle.

In a previous chapter, we discussed the types of runs that Firmino can make to access the penalty area from deep positions. While Mané is more likely to explode at pace into forward areas, Firmino is more nuanced with his movement and we see this here as the Brazilian makes an intelligent run deep into the penalty area that drags opposition players out of position. This creates the opportunity for Salah who is able to break into space as his marker is distracted by Firmino and as the ball is cut back it finds Salah centrally for an easy finish.

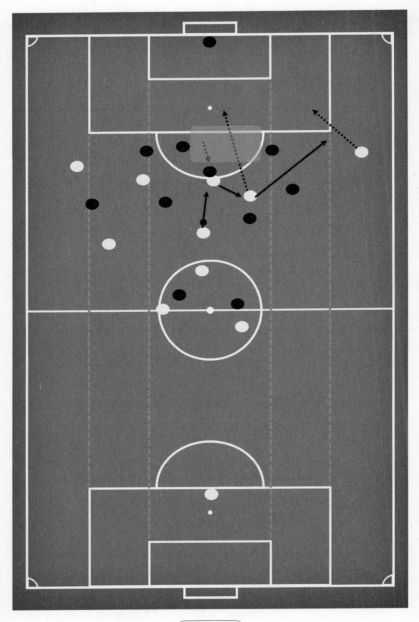

**Figure 82**

## Goal Two: Roberto Firmino vs Leicester City

This time the goal is scored by Roberto Firmino as the Brazilian forward again attacks the penalty area from a deeper area. This time, however, it is Mané and not Firmino who shows for the ball and offers the option for the pass into the final third.

We see the situation developing in *figure 82*. In the central position it was Mané who had been positioned high against the defensive line and Firmino had dropped into a position just to the right of centre. Mané chooses to drop towards the ball to look for the forward pass from Fabinho and this pulls one of the central defenders out to press and engage the potential pass.

As the ball is played forward Mané receives and then lays the pass off to Firmino who is still unmarked. Instead of heading to goal, the Brazilian decides to stretch the defensive line even further with a pass out into the wide area on the right where Alexander-Arnold has advanced into space.

This pass out to the right forces the defensive block to react and to shift across to look to cut off the pass into the area. As the defensive block is moving across Firmino angles his run through the gap in the defensive line and he is in a position to connect with the cross. Once again the key is the positioning in the build-up with players dragging opponents out of position and forcing the defensive block narrow.

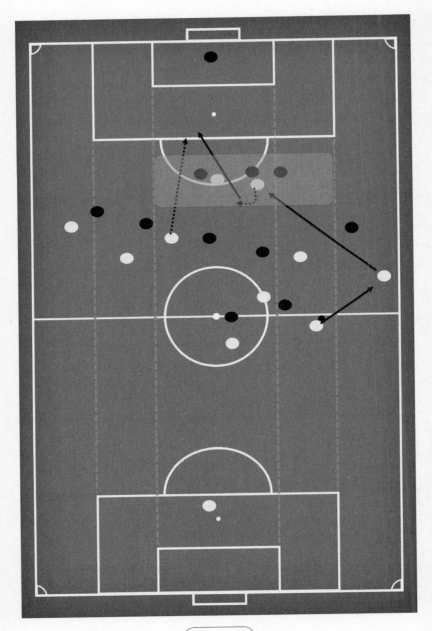

**Figure 83**

## Goal Three: Naby Keïta vs Monterrey

Our third goal showcases the difference in approach that the introduction of Naby Keïta can have in the midfield. We see this goal as it progresses in *figure 83*. Once again the key component of the movement was the positioning of the two forward players in high positions as the play developed. With the ball relatively deep there are two Liverpool players positioned centrally and their positioning has effectively pinned three opposition defenders back.

Initially, the ball is moved wide from the central defender to the right-back. This simple pass moves the ball and changes the angle of the attack. Now the pass to one of the two forward players, Mohamed Salah, is open and the diagonal ball finds Salah to his feet. Normally when Salah receives the ball in these spaces his intent is to spin and attack the space behind the defensive line. This time, though, his initial touch is back towards his own goal.

This touch is the key as it acts as the trigger for Naby Keïta, playing as the left-sided central midfielder, to make an immediate vertical run to access that space behind the defenders. As he does so Salah can simply make the through ball to find the run and Liverpool break through to score.

This is the type of run that the other Liverpool midfielders are less likely to make.

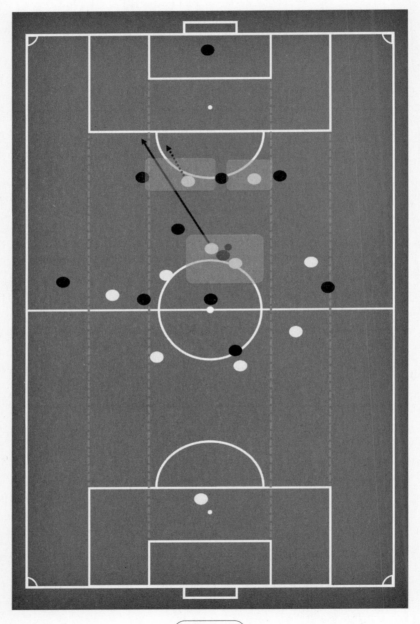

**Figure 84**

## Goal Four: Sadio Mané vs Newcastle

Our fourth goal, shown in *figure 84*, is the first in which our narrative begins with Liverpool out of position and it clearly displays two of the concepts that we have discussed earlier in this book. The first is counter-pressing as with Newcastle in transition with the ball positioned centrally we see two Liverpool players moving forward to engage and press the ball.

These two players forced a turnover and straight away Newcastle, who had been moving forward, were caught out of position. Now we see the importance of the second tactical concept as two Liverpool forwards stayed high and were not active in the press or the defensive transition. When the ball is won back centrally the fact that Mané, to the left of the attack, is still positioned on the highest line and in space allows for the vertical pass through to be played immediately. Mané is able to make the run beyond the defensive line for an easy finish.

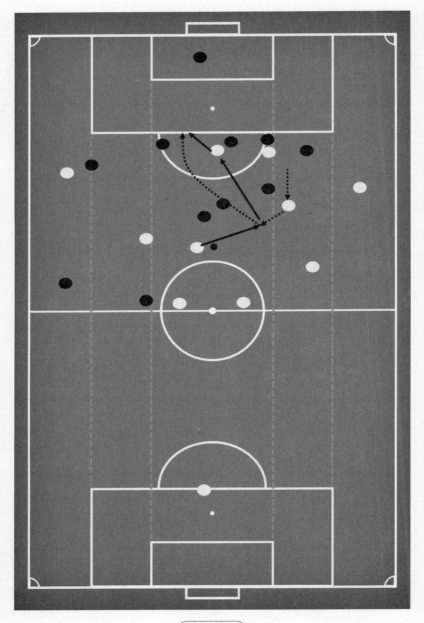

**Figure 85**

## Goal Five: Mohamed Salah vs Newcastle

This goal, shown in *figure 85,* displays the ability of Firmino to play on the highest line while receiving the ball and linking with the attack. Once again we see that Salah is positioned in the half-space and not in the wide areas as he collects possession.

Salah drops into a deeper position to collect possession of the ball ahead of the midfield block of Newcastle. As he does so, as we know the first priority for Liverpool is to play progressively whenever the opportunity presents itself, he plays the ball to the highest line where Firmino is positioned and able to collect possession of the ball.

Firmino takes possession of the ball on the edge of the penalty area and holds off the defender who tries to engage. As soon as Salah had played the pass he followed the ball and when moving at pace from this deeper position he received a flicked pass back from Firmino.

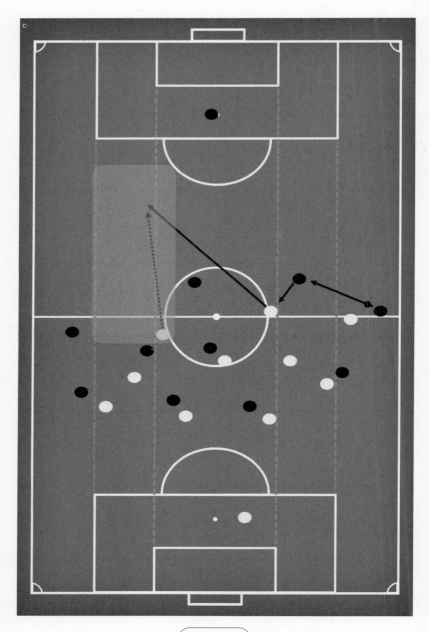

**Figure 86**

## Goal Six: Sadio Mané vs Burnley

In this goal, displayed in *figure 86*, we again see how dangerous Sadio Mané is when moving from deeper positions on the pitch. Burnley are initially in possession of the ball as they try to find a way to play around or through the Liverpool defensive block. Liverpool are positioned well in the defensive phase and there is little space that can be easily accessed by Burnley. Salah is positioned against the left-back who is initially in possession of the ball, and the presence of the Egyptian forces the man in possession to be play the ball back to the central defender.

Here, under little direct pressure, the Burnley defender makes a mistake and plays the pass directly to Firmino.

As the Brazilian takes possession we again see how effective Mané is when moving forward from a deeper position in the half-space. Firmino is able to play the direct pass beyond the defensive line to a line in which Mané can access using his pace.

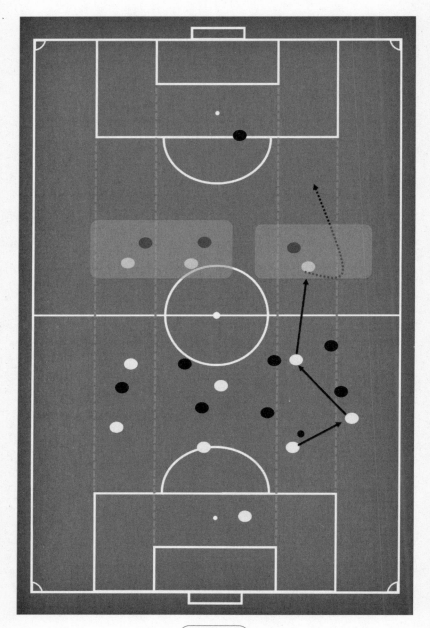

**Figure 87**

## Goal Seven: Mohamed Salah vs Arsenal

The final example in this section is displayed in *figure 87* where we again see what is perhaps the most important tactical concept that Jürgen Klopp employs at Liverpool, with the forward players maintaining a high position when out of possession.

The Arsenal attack had broken down and Liverpool regained possession deep inside their own half of the field. The vertical pass is not immediately open so the ball is moved quickly to the right side and then back to the centre.

These quick diagonal passes play through the initial line of opposition pressure and provide Liverpool with the platform to attack and now the vertical pass is made into the half-space where Salah is positioned.

The key is in the positioning of the front players. While Firmino and Mané are positioned close to one another, Salah is isolated against a single defensive player on the opposite side. The ball is played vertically to Salah and we see his ability to collect the ball and then use his body to roll the defender.

By keeping players on the highest line in this manner we see Liverpool deny the opposition the option of having cover in the backline and in 1v1 situations the Liverpool forwards are deadly.

# Conclusion

Jürgen Klopp is destined to go down in history as one of the best football coaches in football history. His work in his native Germany with FSV Mainz and then with Borussia Dortmund was notable not just because both sides enjoyed great success relative to their expectations at the time but because he left both on such good terms with fans and board alike. Reaching the Champions League Final and winning the Bundesliga title with Dortmund were impressive achievements but they pale in direct comparison to what Klopp has managed to achieve in the English game with Liverpool.

Klopp has been responsible, along with his coaching staff and an excellent recruitment department, for building this Liverpool side in his own image and the success that has followed has been a natural result of that. Liverpool have broken a title drought that stretched far further than anyone could have expected and this is a direct result of the job that Klopp has done at Anfield. The 2018/19 and 2019/20 seasons combined have been incredible for the club on and off the pitch, although they have not always got the trophies that they deserve from these seasons. With no sign that Klopp plans to step away from the club any time soon this success seems set to continue.

From a tactical point of view we have broken down the way that Liverpool progress the ball and the positions that they look to adopt in the final third, along with their performances out of possession with details of the way that the pressing system has changed from when Klopp first arrived in 2015 to now. We have shown the mechanisms that allow players like Sadio Mané and Mohamed Salah to occupy positions that allow them to be amongst the most dangerous forward players in world football and identified the key pivot players who retain central positions and allow other players to move and rotate around them. All of this has been done in the context of the team as a whole, because that is the key to this Liverpool side. They attack and they defend as a unit and the way that the squad has been constructed has allowed Klopp to create a tactical structure that is almost perfectly balanced.

The subjective nature of football is one of the sport's most endearing qualities. You and I could sit side by side to watch a match and take different things away from it depending on the lens through which the game was viewed. My hope is that after reading this book you are now in a position to enjoy the tactical side of the game as much as I do.